IN SPITE OF MOTHER

A SEQUEL

OUT OF MOTHER'S SHADOW
BOOK TWO

LYDIA CONSTANTINE

For permissions please contact the publisher at specrecovery@hotmail.com.

This is a true story, as told by the author, Lydia Constantine. All references to people whether alive or dead, are done using fictional names to protect the privacy of individuals.

Print Paperback ISBN-13: 979-8-9911658-2-2
Print Hardcover ISBN-13: 979-8-9911658-3-9
Printed 2025 Sikeston, MO, USA
Library of Congress Control Number: 2025912845

Book Cover Design and Formatting done by Margaret Daly of RukiaPublishingUS.

PREFACE

I am Lydia and I am 12. I am spending the night with a girlfriend. This was the first time I had ever spent the night with her. We had played games and watched TV until 2 am. We were both asleep. I am a light sleeper and I saw the light from the next room shining through the doorway. I thought it was her aunt checking on us. I open my eyes slightly and see the silhouette of a man coming toward my bed. He bends over me then puts his face down so close to my face, that I can feel his warm breath on my cheek. The strange odor of alcohol is in the air. (I knew it was not bourbon from years of that odor in our house when Dad was an alcoholic.) I feel as though I am frozen and unable to move. I am afraid of what his intentions are and I can feel my heart palpitating in my chest. He says softly "Lydia" and although I hear him, I act as though I am asleep. He says "Lydia" once more and I roll over to my side acting as though I am still asleep. I recognize his voice. He stands there for what seems forever, as though he's trying to make up his mind about something. Finally, he turns and walks to the door. I can see the light from the other room as he opens and closes it. I lift my head to look across the room, to the other bed, where his wife's niece, my girlfriend, is

3

sleeping. I do not know whether she had witnessed this or not. I am relieved but not positive that this is over. My experiences with strange men in movie theaters when I was 9 have made me fearful of all men's intentions. I know this man as a friend of my parents and am relieved that he has walked out.

It's after 2 am and I am so exhausted that even this traumatic experience couldn't keep me awake. Sleeping was no escape. I dreamed that I was running through a large building with someone chasing me. I looked back to see if I knew who it was and heard this man calling my name. I could not make out the face to determine whether or not it was the same man that was in the bedroom. I see a large door, run through it and slam it in his face! Looking for a way to escape, I see a small window that I think I can get through, but hope the man is too big to follow me. As I reach the window, he comes into the room, and I cannot get the window to open. He starts to grab me and I throw myself through the plate glass window! I see his arm reaching through to grab me as I roll onto my feet to start running again. I look down and there is blood all over me. At this point, I woke up frightened! I sat up then looked around the room, but there was no one in sight except my girlfriend who was sound asleep. I look at my body for the blood. Then I realized that I had been dreaming and laid back down. I couldn't wait for daylight so I could go home.

I dozed off and once again a dream surfaced that I had dreamed many times. In the dream, I was about 6 years old and the dream always began with looking through the window at the pouring rain. Large mud puddles formed, on the dirt road, outside my father's tractor business, where numerous pieces of equipment had traveled back and forth making large holes. I loved to put on my father's knee boots and wade those large puddles.

I went to the closet and pulled out his boots. They would fit me like hip boots and my feet would barely touch the bottoms.

In some spots, the water was so deep it would come up over halfway on the boots. I sat down in the dirt to put them on then turned over to push myself up with my hands. I began to walk in the water but I started feeling something moving inside the boot! I hastened to get out of the water but before I could reach land, a large snake followed by several small snakes came slithering out of both boots! (In my repetitive dreams of the past, this was where the dream always ended.) But not this time! In my attempt to get out of the boots, I fell into the water. I struggled to get to land, as I could not see where the snakes had fallen in, due to the churning, mucky color of the puddle. I began feeling sharp bites on my legs and feet! I sat up in the bed and screamed which brought both my friend's aunt and uncle running into the room. They flipped on the light switch which awakened my friend.

Her aunt said, "Lydia, are you alright?" I stared directly into the eyes of her uncle and said, "I had the most horrible nightmare!" The aunt said, "What was it about?" I could see the fear in his eyes and realized he was afraid of what I was going to say. I hesitated for a few moments, then said, "Something from my past that I cannot recall. Perhaps I will remember later. If I do, I will let you know. I'm so sorry I woke you all up."

I always thought these nightmares are just remnants from the past when I was a little girl. Hopefully, they were not premonitions of things to come. Let's go back to where my previous story, "Mother's Little Alibi" stopped and continue the journey. Perhaps we'll soon find out the source of these nightmares.

CHAPTER 1

LYDIA MOVES ON

Being unsure of where to begin the rest of my story, I'll start where I left off in 1954 when the gunfight in December almost killed me.

At age 11, after our traumatic Christmas, I moved to another state with my mother, who was anticipating her divorce. I had hoped I had experienced the last time of being left alone while mother pursued her own interests. January of 1955 I was enrolled in a school down the street from an apartment Mother had rented. I would walk home after school and open the door with a hidden key, then lock the door behind me and do my homework, practice my flute, or read a book until mother came home from her bank job.

I had started playing the flute, anticipating being in the junior high band next year. The music teacher had sent a note home with me today, stating that the music students would be going to the high school one day next week. We would take our instruments and play with the current jr. high band. The note also said the parents should pick us up at 4pm at the high school, which was 3 or 4 miles from our home. The town was considerably larger than the small one I had grown up in. When Mother came home at 4 o'clock, I handed her the note, and she seemed to be okay with this.

On the morning I was to be picked up at the high school, I left for school with my flute, unconcerned about the pick-up. Mother left for work, while I walked to school. We were loaded into a bus that afternoon a little before 2 then taken to the high school. It was fun to play the instruments with the older kids, and when the practice was over a few minutes before 4, everyone went out to look for their parents. I looked around for Mother and could not see her car anywhere. I had not attended the school long enough to know someone whose parents might have offered me a ride. As the minutes flew by, everyone had left so I was wondering what to do. I thought she would be there shortly as she finished work at 4pm.

I sat down on the steps and waited, but I couldn't stay long because the sun was going down, making the air colder. I had been asked earlier by a teacher if I had a ride, and I answered, "Yes" because I believed I did. At that time, girls were not allowed to wear long pants to school, only dresses so my legs were getting really cold. My hands were also about to freeze because I had forgotten my mittens. It was impossible to put my hands in my pockets, because I was carrying my flute and my books. The cold wind was making my eyes water. I had to figure out something to do soon.

I looked down the street at the direction we had come from in the bus, then decided I would try to walk home. The school was on a long street with nothing but trees behind it. Across from that street were several other streets that ran all the way to the main thoroughfare. I just kept walking on this street because I thought if Mother came, she would probably see me walking, since it was very straight and you could see a long distance. It was getting darker, and I was very apprehensive about being lost in this large town. Several cars passed in both directions. Some of them would slow down, which worried me that they might try to grab me off the street. I tried to walk faster, so I would appear to know where I was going. This one car had been by me once moving slowly and now it had turned around to come back. It was a man driving, and he pulled up beside me and said, "It's awfully cold, do you need a ride?"

I looked down the next street and saw an old man and old women unloading groceries and carrying them up their stairs into their house. I said, "No, I'm on my way to my grandparents and they just live down this street." I pointed to the couple and he turned to look at them. He drove off quickly. I started to run toward the couple, because I feared they would go into their house, then they might not answer their door. (I had good luck years before with old people I did not know, taking me in out of the rain, when I was left behind. That thought encouraged me to try to do it again.) I was yelling, "Mister, can you help me, please?" He and his wife stopped, then he turned and asked me what I needed I told him who I was, then explained that I been forgotten. His wife said, "You must be frozen, your cheeks are flame red." They invited me to come into the house to warm up, while we all tried to figure out some way to contact my mother.

I was thinking that Mother might be with her boyfriend and that they we might not be able to find her. I knew the name of the bank where she worked. They called but it was already closed. I did not know our apartment address, but I knew the address of the school. The man put me in the car and drove to the school. From there I guided him to my house. When we arrived, the lights were on, but no one was home. I thought Mother was probably looking for me. I retrieved the key. The old man went in the apartment and sat with me until she returned. When she finally stormed into the house, she was very upset because I had let a man, I did not know bring me home. This started a heated discussion, between them, regarding how I had been left alone. He told her he had considered taking me to the police department, but was afraid no one would look for me there. She asked him where he had found me, and he explained the situation.

At that point Mother said she remembered the band pick-up but was just late from work. She apologized to him, and I thanked him before he left. The minute he walked out the door, she started yelling at me about leaving the school grounds. She said she had come to get me at 4 and was late and when she didn't see me, she waited at the school to see if I would come out later. I knew this was not true because you could see the front of the school all of the way down to the street I turned on to go to the old people's home. She must have come by home first because the lights were on when I arrived. And when I looked at the clock in the couple's house, it was after 5. I never knew if she had gone out with her boyfriend again or if she truly was late. Usually, it would have been the former. That night I was too tired to care. I was emotionally upset and just wanted to eat, do homework and go to bed. Mother sat down and spent the evening talking on the phone to her boyfriend. I wanted to go home and wondered how much longer Daddy would be gone taking the alcohol cure, and if I would ever see him again.

CHAPTER 2

DESIRE FOR A NORMAL FAMILY

When Daddy was to return from the Alcohol Cure program, Mother and I were already at the house waiting. When she and I stepped into the house that day, we saw it was exactly as it was when we had escaped. The debris from the shotgun was on the floor. The shredded tablecloth and pad were still there, and the far wall was imbedded with the "pellets" from the shotgun.

She told me to sit down in the living room to wait. When he walked in the door, I ran to him and he picked me up and hugged me the tightest he ever had. Mother just stood there. He walked up to her, kissed her on the cheek, grabbed me by the hand and walked toward the living room. Walking through the dining room he looked at where the buckshot had ended up in the wall after he had shot at us. Mother had thrown away the tablecloth and the shredded mat that covered the table before he got home. You could see that he was visibly upset about the wall. I tried not to notice the wall and how distressed it made him. It brought back scary moments to me and I couldn't wait until the wall was repaired. As I grew older, when it was getting dark, I could not walk through that room as it scared me. I would walk down the hall instead. I never liked that room again and dreaded family meals at the table.

Daddy had not been in the house after the state patrol arrested him that night. He had been sent to jail and upon his release, he selected to go to the Alcohol Cure Program in a city, 150 miles away. He was not allowed to return home before leaving town. Nothing had been done to the house because Mother packed our things that night and we went to another town to stay in a hotel until she found a job and an apartment. Her boyfriend lived in that town so we went out to eat with him in the evenings. I don't know what they were thinking. It was as though I didn't exist. Maybe because I was a child, they didn't think I knew what was going on. Maybe they didn't care what I thought. I cared a lot! I loved my Daddy and wanted to go back home and be a family like the other families I knew in town. Those dreams were so evasive and seemed as though they were about to end.

Daddy sat down on the sofa and asked Mother to come sit down, too. She did, but in the chair across from the sofa. I sat down next to Daddy. He started out by telling both of us how sorry he was for what he had done. He said he now realized how close he had come to killing us both. He had written the same thing in multiple letters to Mother and me from the cure center. He begged us to forgive him and he cried. I already had forgiven him, so I told him he was forgiven and I cried, too. He also told us that he did not want a divorce, and he would never drink another drop of alcohol if she would drop the divorce proceedings. Her only words were, "I will think about it and let you know tomorrow." She was very sullen and did not shed a tear.

I didn't sleep much that night for worrying about what Mother would decide. I did not want to continue living a life with her seeing her boyfriend and leaving me alone. I did not like the man. When Daddy was sober, he was a good father. I was afraid if she left him, he would go back to drinking. Then I might not have been allowed to see him because he was drunk and considered dangerous since the shooting. I hoped that she would forgive him and give up her boyfriend. If Daddy was strong enough to give up alcohol for us, why couldn't she give up that man for us? I went to bed in my bedroom, Daddy went to bed in their bedroom, and mother stayed in the guest room and locked the door.

When the next morning finally came, I was in my pajamas and got out of the bed as soon as they got up. Mother had been sleeping in the guest room and when she came out, she had been crying. We all sat down at the kitchen table. Mother immediately said she had decided not to divorce now. She would stay married to him as long as he didn't start drinking again. However, she said as soon as I left home for college, she was going to get a divorce. Daddy said he would accept those terms as he was a changed man. He told me that hopefully by the time I left home, he could have changed her mind. She did not seem pleased with that remark. I was so happy I couldn't eat my breakfast. I really was about to have a normal family.

I was excited about being back in school with my same teacher and all of my friends. Everyone, especially Edith seemed excited to see me. I began to think about having friends over to spend the night. No one was ever able to come over before, because Daddy was always drunk while Mother was always gone. Mother still went out at night, but Daddy was there with me and sober.

My best friend Edith was the first to come stay. I had spent many nights at her house in the past. She had a large family plus an aunt that lived with them. Both her mom and dad worked so the aunt prepared all the meals and kept the house. It was such a treat to get up for breakfast in that household. Her aunt would make the best French toast and I always looked forward to the invitation. We would play duets on the piano, games outside in the yard and board games. When she came to my house, she wanted to watch TV as they did not have one at their house.

On one of the stays at Ediths, her oldest sister came home from college with a new product she had found in the city. She had given one to Edith to take to my house for supper. It was a Chef Boyardee Pizza package. It had the ingredients for the dough for the crust, pizza sauce and shredded cheese in a can. You could add what meat you wanted and at that time ham was very popular since there was no Pepperoni available in a small town. We made it, and it was wonderful! It was our first pizza! It wasn't anything like the pizzas to come later, but we had nothing else similar to compare it to, so it was the best.

Aunt Ann, who was my mother's sister, Edith and her family and Girl Scouts provided the strength I needed to survive the early 50's. Aunt Ann was my mentor. Edith was my rock, as she supported me regardless of how bad or good I was. Girl Scouts provided the entertainment and camaraderie I needed in a mundane world.

CHAPTER 3

GIRL SCOUT CAMP

GIRL SCOUT CAMP

This is a trip down "memory lane" for thousands of young girls that are now grown. Anyone who experienced camping as a child during the 1950's will relate to the low comfort level we experienced without all the amenities we have today. One of the greatest pleasures of my young life was going to Girl Scout camp with my best friend, Edith. She was always willing to try anything that I wanted to do even though some of them were not the wisest. Girl Scout Camp was one of the better ones. Edith and I started going to camp at about the age of 8. We were driven to the camp the first time, which was situated on a lake about 65 miles from our home, by my mother. Mother had already told everybody in town that I was probably not going to be able to spend time away from home without being homesick. Where she got that idea, I'll never know. It was a pleasure for me, anytime that I could escape the turmoil of the drinking and infidelity at home. Until that time, the only break I had received in the past was the times I had spent with Aunt Ann, or overnighting at

Edith's. Now that I am 12, I am reminiscing about the first time I came to camp.

I remembered when we arrived at the camp the very first time. Edith and I were shown the meeting hall where we would have our meals. On the wall was a circle called a "Kaper Chart" with an arrow in the middle that you could spin. Written on it were the words: Color Guard, Shoppers, Wood Gatherers, Fire starters, Cooks, Clean-up, and Latrine. Each girl would spin it, and this determined your chores for the day. My first spin landed on Latrine. It wasn't until the next day that I found out that latrine meant they were talking about an "outhouse." I would have to empty lime into the latrine holes (2 holes in each one) and clean the seats with Pine Sol cleaner. We had a maid/cook at home and an indoor toilet so I had never done any of these things before. Edith had her aunt, who lived with them to do these chores. We looked at each other, but neither said a word. It was too late, there was no going back now. I looked around at the other girls who were here for the first year and could see that some of them were having second thoughts, about the "fun" week ahead. I couldn't go home because Mother would say "I told you so," and Edith would probably have left with me ruining her camping experience.

There was a green cup in the middle of the table, where we dined, with tongue depressors in it. Written on them were the words: Get water, clean silverware, clean cups, clean plates, sweep around table, and the word Hopper. (The Hopper's job was to run back and forth to the kitchen for things that someone needed that wasn't on the table.)

Different ages were assigned to different campsites. The campsites had great names like Shady Oak which was for the youngest girls. If you came again, you would be assigned to Hickory Hollow, then Gypsy Dell and the oldest girls went to Pioneer, which was tents on wood platforms instead of screened cabins like the younger girls stayed in.

Edith and I entered the Shady Oak cabin and looked at the beds lined up against the wall. There was no way to keep dry if it rained because the head of the beds were right below the screened in area of the walls. We had been given an oil cloth, which was waterproof, to lay over the bed during the day in case it rained. We would have to move our beds as close together in the middle of the room as we could, in order to stay dry, if the rain came at night. There was no ceiling fan to cool you, so you were dependent upon Mother Nature to keep you cool at night. Some nights not a single breeze moved a leaf on the trees around us. The humidity hung over us like a cake cover, encompassing the whole cabin. We'd go to sleep with no cover on us and wake in the middle of the night, freezing. You'd pull up the quilt that you had brought with you and sleep the rest of the night.

Edith and I put our suitcases under the bed then went to a place called a Trading Post. We took money that our parents had given us to spend and left it there. If you wanted to purchase an item there, you would go in to pick it out, then they would subtract money from your account to pay for it. This was the same place we had been to when we arrived to register for camp. We had been introduced to the nurse and the rest of the staff.

On our first evening, we went for supper and we all lined up for the flag ceremony. The color guard had red ribbons put on their shirts to identify them. Their job was to take the flag down and to fold it up properly. Following that a bugler played "Taps" then we lined up to enter the hall for supper. We said Grace, which was usually the" Johnny Appleseed" version, which is "The Lord is good to me and so I thank the Lord, for giving me, the things I need, the Sun, the Rain and the apple seed, the Lord is good to me. Amen." We then started our duties to serve dinner and clean up.

Afterwards, we would meet around a campfire and sit on a square cloth that had been made at our Girl Scout meetings at home. It consisted of two pieces of "oil cloth" which was water-

17

proof with newspaper between them. You sewed it around the edges, then rolled it up, tied it and carried it with us to use for sitting purposes. They were called "sit-upons" which I thought was an appropriate name. At night we would make a circle around a campfire and sing songs. Someone would tell stories, stand up and make gestures to take us on a "Bear Hunt". This involved physical movements we all made to tell the story. The campfire's purpose would help to deter the mosquitoes, but a few always bit you anyway.

When it was bedtime, some of those happy girls we had played with during the day became sad. Some were homesick but trying not to show it. They would become very quiet. There was little laughing at this hour of the day. A couple of them broke down and started crying and asking why they couldn't go home. One was crying, as though she was being tortured. She wanted her Momma and finally she made so much noise during what had been called our "quiet time." that one of the counselors came into the cabin to try to console her. The rest of us were told to go to sleep, which was difficult with the crying, talking, consoling and nose blowing going on. We all wanted to hear what was going to happen to her, so we had our eyes closed, but we were all listening. They finally convinced her to go to sleep by telling her they would call her mother in the morning, if she still wanted to go home.

The next morning, she had her things all thrown in a bag ready to go. The counselor told her to wait in the cabin as they had called her mother and she was on her way. We were present when her mother got there. I cannot say that her mother was excited to see her as she was to see her mother. I imagine that mother had just began to enjoy time to herself until now when it had been cut short by a bad case of homesickness. The rest of the girls moping about going home last night had supposedly gotten over their being homesick, so we got dressed and prepared for the day.

Every morning at camp, the counselors would get us up early by ringing a very loud bell. We would get dressed then line up for the flag ceremony. The color guard would put the flag back up, and we would say the "Pledge of Allegiance". Following that, we went to the dinner hall and had our breakfast using the same routine as the evening meal. A friend of mine said the only thing she remembered about the meals is that they always had a lot of prunes for breakfast. It worried her that they thought we all had serious bowel problems, since only old people she knew ate prunes daily.

There was an old home, called the" Old House," where we did crafts in the mornings. One craft required was the making of a lanyard. It was a very colorful woven necklace that was adjustable, and you put a silver hook on the end of it so you might add a whistle. Some of us took longer than others to make it. I was one of those people. We started on this project the first day and 4 days later, I had this strange thing with straps hanging every direction but looked nothing like what the others had. Edith was better at following directions, and even with her help, I could not master it. I was still working on mine the day before we left to go home. I was becoming concerned that it might keep me from being released the next day, so I was really focused on it. I was beginning to panic! Perhaps, I thought this is something I had to do before they would consider me finished with this experience. I might have to stay another week. One of the counselors took pity on me the last day and with her helping me, I finally finished it.

For lunch every day we were required to cook our own meals. The girls who had drawn "shoppers" had to retrieve the ingredients for the meals we were preparing. Neither Edith nor I were particularly good at this either, but we had mastered hot dogs and s'mores in record time. Following our lunch, we were sent back to the cabins to rest. They called this the "Horizontal Hour." We were all too hot to nap so we read books or whispered to each other until we were allowed up again. After rest, we would all go to swim in the lake.

At the lake, there was a board on a post, which had hooks that held numbers. You were to take one of the numbers and hang it on the other side of the board to indicate you were in the water. They called this the "Buddy System" because a second person picked the number next to it and moved it to the other side. You were to remember each other's number. Every once in a while, they would tell you to go to your buddy which was to verify that you both were still above water. Those who did not know how to swim, were gathered together to learn, and the rest of us just swam around and played in the water until they told us to get out. When you stepped on dry land, you were to go to the board and move your number back to the other side, to indicate you were out of the water.

Swimming was the only bathing I did for the whole week. Were it not for the swimming water, it might have been difficult to stay in the same cabin with me. As an only child, I was very modest and refused to undress and get in a shower with 3 other girls. I even dressed under the sheets in my bed. The counselors would stay outside the shower area, to make sure everyone used it. I would take my towel, go in and stick my head under the shower head. I would then wait a few minutes and walk out with a wet head, carrying a damp towel. There must have been few only children in my group because everybody else, stripped off all their clothes and showered. They all looked at me as though I was very strange, but I didn't care. I saw all age girls with hair in lots of different places that I didn't have it, and I was embarrassed for them and me. On my first trip, no one had told me about girl's body changes. This was my first intro to sexual education. I started looking at my body every day after that for fear hair was growing some place on me! Some of them had big breasts and some had none. Neither tried to cover them up which I thought I would have done if I looked like that.

Somedays we had archery and other days we went hiking. Hiking caused me lots of problems as I was extremely allergic to Poison Ivy. Edith reminded me that much of the week, I was painted pink with Calamine lotion, which didn't help that much. When I got hot at night, it itched worse. The only other things that were scary at camp were the free-range animals. Cows and wild hogs were pests looking for food that wasn't put away properly. Snakes are always a problem, especially the venomous ones. Copperheads were common in this area. You were likely to run into snakes or the wild hogs if you left the pathways through the woods. The cows were large but not a threat. My only bad encounter was with ants. I was sitting around a campfire late in the day with my legs crossed wearing short shorts. Several ants crawled into my underwear and I had no choice but to jump up and run to the latrine. Some of them were biting me. I stripped out of my shorts and underwear and killed them. I put my panties and shorts back on then went back and looked at my "sit upon." When I picked it up there were ants everywhere. I shook it off and found a new place to sit. This gave me a whole new attitude about the term "ants in your pants".

This last trip in 1955, left me in a melancholy mood. I, like a lot of other girls, loved Girl Scout camp. Sadly, there is no longer a summer camp at this lake that we attended. I would have loved for my great granddaughters to have experienced it. There is nothing on the internet that can duplicate a real- life experience in the outdoors. It helped you to be self- sufficient and work as a team, as well as have a lot of fun with the other girls that you had befriended. The Latrine, not so much fun, especially if you drew that job more than once like I did.

CHAPTER 4

THE CHEMISTRY SET

There was a new boy my age, named Willard that had moved near us. He was a lot of fun and very mischievous. When Christmas came the year that I turned 12, he said why don't you ask for a Gilbert Chemistry Set? When I asked why, he said we can make stink bombs and all kinds of things that would be fun to do, but my parents won't let me have one. That should have told me that there was a reason he was not getting a chemistry set. After I saw it in the catalog, I decided it might be fun. At this point I want to mention that the toy industry was not restricted in 1955 for fear of purchasers hurting themselves. Even though it's primary customers would be age 10- 18. Makers of Chemistry sets did not worry about chemicals, flammable potions, Bunsen burners, using a match to light things, or a host of other dangers that would be deemed highly inappropriate for a 12- year- old to do by themselves. One of the children's sets was called Atomic and actually contained radioactive uranium ore, and a blow torch for glassmaking. My parents said "absolutely not" to that one. We decided on the beginner set.

In our house we had a second story accessible by a pull-down -stairs. Mother said that if I got the chemistry set, I would have to use it upstairs, as she was very fastidious and did not want me to make a mess with the bottles in one of the rooms downstairs.

On Christmas Day, when I received my gift, she wouldn't let me open the box after I removed the Christmas paper. She had Daddy take a card table and chairs upstairs, along with the chemistry set. Later that day Willard came over and we opened up everything in it. This included alcohol for the Bunsen burner, litmus paper, test tubes, assorted chemicals in glass bottles and a box of matches. There was an instruction book telling us how to make various things and a page in the back titled "Precautions" which mentioned adult supervision if we were younger children. We were not nearly as interested in the Precautions, so we ignored that page and since the box had not been opened in front of my parents they never saw it. After all, I was upstairs and our only interest was the things we could produce.

I read the book and then gave it to Willard to read. He immediately started talking about stink bombs that we could put in places to make people run outside. He thought one of the local movie theaters would be a great place for one. I was reluctant to agree with him, but later that month, we did make one, and he took it home in a bottle. He had also told me he had read in some book about getting soup and heating it in the can. You opened it, took it to the balcony of a movie theater, and emptied it while it was warm. At the same time, you poured it out over the audience, you made a sound like you were throwing up.

He ran both of these options past me and I suggested that if he used the soup idea, he would probably be caught before he could get down the steps to the first floor. We only had one movie theater with a balcony in town. If we were caught, we probably would never be able to attend that theater again. I knew I also would be punished with Mother's switch in addition to the excommunication from the movies had I done that. I did not know Willard's family discipline practices so I asked him what would happen to him. He said he was not a "fraidy-cat" like me and was brave enough to stand up to a paddling.

I moved the conversation back to the stink bomb and what we could do with it. He said he could use it in the other movie theater in town. He would go to the front row where all the kids sat and open the bottle. He would then run out with all the others, and no one would know it was him. I told him that everyone would think it was me, as it was all over town that I got the chemistry set for Christmas that could make stink bombs. He did make the stink bomb and took it home with him. He later let it loose in the movie theater and got caught. After that, he lost his interest in the chemistry set and me. His getting in trouble at the theater could have played a big part in that. I'm sure he told his parents it was my fault, and they now considered me an unsuitable playmate.

I was home alone a lot since we no longer had the full- time maid and babysitter. I knew Willard wasn't coming back. One day when I was all alone and bored, I went upstairs to find out what you could do with a chemistry set that might be fun. Even though I no longer had a "cohort in crime" to share the exploits I looked through the book for something different to do. I had tried a few experiments on my own after Willard quit coming over, and had used up a lot of the bottles of chemicals that were part of the set. After reading one of the experiments that I still had components to complete, I decided to try it. This involved lighting my Bunsen burner, which I had not done very often. The small bottle that held the alcohol needed to be refilled. As I was pouring the alcohol in, I spilled a small amount on the table. We had always used old newspapers to cover the card table so we would not ruin the surface, and it soaked into those papers. When I put the top that contained the wick on, the paper looked dry so I thought everything would be alright. I struck a match to light the wick, but apparently it had not soaked enough alcohol up to light it. I kept holding the match trying to light it, and it burned my finger which caused me to drop the match and immediately the newspapers flamed up! I was in a state of panic! There was no one there to help me and no water upstairs! I looked around and saw the drapes on the window. I yanked one down and turned around to put it on the fire, but the flames were higher so I doubled up the drape and attempted to put the fire out. The drape began to smoke so I removed it and stomped it with my feet. After a bit, the flame was gone, and I thought it was done. What a relief!

About that time, I heard Daddy yelling at me. He said "Where are you? I smell smoke!" I looked down the stairwell and started crying and told him what I had done. He rushed upstairs carrying some water just as the drape reignited. He put it out and looked around. He looked at me and said, "Lydia, pack up the Chemistry Set while I get something to put the drape and burned things into. I think you've burned a hole in the card table, so fold it up and we'll bring it downstairs, too." When everything was carried out, he said, "I am putting the Chemistry Set in the burn barrel. I'm sorry, but it is too dangerous to leave in the house. Now go open all the windows upstairs to let the smoke out." As I climbed the stairs for the last time, I had already decided that chemistry was not for me, so I cannot say that I was disappointed.

CHAPTER 5

TELEVISION IN THE COUNTRY

In the spring that year I turned 13. Mother and Daddy seemed to be getting along and life was good. Mother started a new routine. Several nights a week she would go to town to meet a "girlfriend" leaving Daddy and me at the house. He never questioned her and would never have gone to town himself. After his cure from alcohol, he was embarrassed by his past and never set foot in the town until after Mother's death. His business was outside of town and that was as far toward town as he went. His few friends and relatives always came to his house to visit.

When Mother was gone, Daddy would play games or cards with me and watch TV. That wonderful TV that I saw in California in 1949 with the black and white screen had finally made it to the Midwest in the early 1950's. The only problem was the nearest tv station was 150 miles away. Daddy's solution was to put up a tall antenna on the roof of our farm house. There was a box you set on the top of the tv that had a dial that controlled the direction the antenna moved to pick up a signal. If you were lucky you could see the images on the set through the heavy "snow." In 1954 a local station was opened 50 miles away which made the picture not perfect but a lot better. The station would start early in the morning with the national anthem and late in the evening would sign off. The rest of the night you could look at the signal pattern on the screen but nothing else.

On September 9, 1956, Elvis Presley was scheduled to appear on the Ed Sullivan Show, and I invited Edith to the house to watch it. We were so excited and had talked about it all week. Daddy teased us about how he wasn't sure the TV antenna control on top of the house could work with all the wild moves Elvis would be making. Edith and I were so excited when he came on stage. He sang "Don't Be Cruel" and "You Ain't Nothing but a Hound Dog." The TV channel faded in and out, but his singing was heard the whole time, as we still had the volume. We were bouncing up and down on the sofa as he became visible in all the "snow," and then we would settle down as he faded away again. This happened over and over again but we were "glued" to the set so we wouldn't miss anything that might show up. We would have been as emotional as all those young girls we saw on TV, but the reception coming in from the antenna showed a wavering body, then nothing then a body, etc. This put a damper on all our teenage emotions. TV brought a whole new world to the teenage population, especially in the rural areas where seeing Elvis in person would have been an impossibility.

CHAPTER 6

DADDY, THE ENTREPRENEUR

This was also the year that Daddy's entrepreneurial spirit returned. There was a piece of farmland in the middle of a big plantation and the river, that he wanted to buy. He planned to have it farmed by a sharecropper. He had moved a man and his family into a house of the farm where we lived. This man farmed the land we already owned for a "share" of the crop plus lived in his house rent free.

Daddy had money to invest from his previous investments, the income from the farm he already owned debt free, and his improving farm equipment business. Mother had played a big part in making a profit in farm equipment, and managing to save it during his sick and alcoholic years. So, she expected to have a say in this new venture.

He put a down payment on the farm and then told Mother he was buying it. That was a mistake! He should have told her and explained how he was going to pay for it first. Having had such a sad life after her father blew all their money on farmland that was worthless, Mother was easily upset with anything that might jeopardize their financial security.

I had just come from school, and they were fighting at the

business. Daddy had locked the front door because he did not want anyone to come in and hear this fight. When he let me in, he was trying to explain to her how they could pay for the farm with the income off the farm he was purchasing, and off of the farm that was paid for if they had to have additional money. This was not consoling to her. She didn't understand it, or didn't want to appear to understand. She screamed at him about how she had worked her butt off to get the finances where they were today. She didn't want to go in debt again. This argument continued the rest of the afternoon, all the way home, through dinner with her throwing the pots and pans around and breaking a dish or two.

My stomach was in knots by bedtime, when Daddy had gone to bed, and she had sat down in the rocking chair by his bed to started rocking and crying. She would cry a little, threaten divorce, tell him he didn't love her, how ungrateful he was for the work she had done to make it successful, etc. He would roll over or sit up and try to explain, but she never listened. This went on all night. I finally fell asleep, but when I woke up the next morning, she was still at it. Regardless, Daddy bought the farm, and she was happy later that he did. I was just happy that the signing for the farm went through that day, so I could get some sleep that night. If this was what a normal family was like, I wasn't sure it was part of my ideal dreams of normalcy. Being an entrepreneur in his case was hard on his family life. As for me, I always worried when she brought up divorce again.

CHAPTER 7

AUSTIN AND THE LITTLE RED WAGON

Still, I have always been a fan of entrepreneurs, but the youngest and most brazen one I ever met was 12 years old. His name was Austin. My Daddy had a large lot behind his farm equipment business. In the 1950's they used a combine pulled behind a tractor to harvest crops. That combine was called a "pull-type" and the grains came in the front, then the threshed grain came out the back. After the grain was threshed it would be dumped into a burlap bag. A man riding on a platform on the side of the combine would stitch the top of the bag and slide it off the combine. This was a very intense job, bagging and catching it. The later models replaced the bagging with an auger and grain bin which allowed them to dump it into a wagon to be hauled off. Dad's equipment franchise came out with one of the first "self-propelled" combines that had a grain tank built on top of it and required no tractor to pull it. Lots of farmers were trading in their "pull-type." to exchange for the new "self-propelled" combines. This left a lot of the trade-ins setting inside the fence behind the business, where they were highly unlikely to be purchased with the new technology available. Additionally, there was a lot of discarded scrap metal that had no place to go that was dumped all around the inside of the fence.

Austin was from a poor family, but he was very enterprising. At the age of 12 he had asked my dad if he might have some of that scrap metal along the fence. Dad knew the family and their financial plight, and there wasn't a lot he could carry off in his little red wagon, so he said, "Yes.".

Most of the scrap material was hidden from view since it was mostly behind the building, where lots of tall weeds had grown up. There was no way to see what was going on in the fenced area, unless you were back there looking for something. Sometimes Daddy would "rob" a part a farmer was looking for from the combines. That farmer would be one who was still using the "pull-type". It was getting harder to buy parts for it, as the years went by and that combine was becoming obsolete.

No one was checking to see what Austin was carrying off or how often he was coming. We were not sure where he took the salvage to sell. One day, a large truck and trailer pulled up and drove between the business and the old grocery store that used to be our home. There was a large gate that opened into the lot where the combines were. Daddy was in the office so he did not see this truck. A customer walked in the building about an hour later and said, "So you're finally getting rid of those old rusty combines." Daddy said "No, I'm keeping them because I still have some customers who need parts off of them." The customer said "Well there's a big truck and trailer loading one of them right now."

Daddy rushed out and asked the driver what he thought he was doing with this combine he was loading. The driver told him he needed to talk to the young man who had brought them there to pick it up. Daddy turned around and saw Austin walking around another combine, with a man from the salvage yard in the enclosure. He yelled at him to explain what was going on. Austin said, "I'm taking the combines to the salvage. I have hauled off all the small pieces from around the fence and these are all that is left."

Daddy was speechless! He turned to the driver and said, "What would make you think that a kid would be able to sell you these combines?" The driver said, "He has been bringing salvage to our place for over 6 months. When he started, he told us that Mr. Lyle told him he could have anything he could haul off inside the fence."

Austin said, "Mr. Lyle these combines are inside the fence so I thought I could have them too." Daddy thought for a few minutes and said, "Austin, I was talking about the small items all along the fence, not a combine. Things you might haul off in your little red wagon. I am sorry that we have this misunderstanding, but I am going to write you a check, so that you may pay these people for making the trip, and I will give you some extra money. If we have any other small scrap metal put out there again, you are still welcome to it." Then he turned to the driver and told him to unload the combine. Begrudgingly, the driver and his helper put the combine back inside the fence. They didn't offer Austin a ride home. He stood there looking forlorn, holding Daddy's check in his hand. He had settled his debt with the driver, and he reluctantly headed for home. Daddy said to the farmer who had watched this whole encounter, "Thank God, the combines wouldn't fit in the little red wagon."

CHAPTER 8

THE TEEN YEARS START

In my 13th year, I began to put on weight. It seems like everything tasted good to me, and I was eating 3 meals a day plus a snack. The school lunch program was fabulous. They cooked the meals at the school, and we had homemade yeast rolls plus great entrees as well as desserts. I never passed up anything that was offered to me. It was nothing like today's school cafeteria where you have a choice about what you ate. What they put on my plate was my meal. I didn't realize how chubby I had become from the lack of discipline in my food intake, as my parents never said anything about it. I was 5'3" tall and 142 pounds when they finally weighed me.

A friend invited me to a birthday party where her dad took pictures. We were all standing behind the birthday cake table for the blowing out of the candles. Her Father had a picture made for each of us to have. When I received the picture from him, I was shocked! Here I was twice as wide as some of the other girls. What really embarrassed me was the picture showed everyone looking at the camera except for me. I was looking at the cake!

I went home and cried about it, but did not say anything to my parents. I waited until the next weekend when I went to Aunt

Ann's (my mother's only sister), where I told her about it. Aunt Ann had a problem maintaining her weight all her life. During the process of my pouring my heart out about my fat little body, she walked out of the room. I thought "How mean, she doesn't care either!" I resumed my pity party with one big tear running down my face. Raising my dress to wipe my nose on my slip, (a habit I had acquired when mother told me to quit wiping my nose on my sleeve, but instead to always carry a handkerchief). I never did manage to remember the handkerchief. Mother was none the wiser about the slip as she was probably checking the sleeves. When Aunt Ann returned, she was carrying a small paper pamphlet that was about the size of a man's wallet. She said, "This is a healthy diet." If you will do the things they tell you to do and eat what they tell you to eat, you will be thin like your Mother Ava, instead of overweight like your Aunt Ann.

She hugged me and told me this would be our little secret. She sent me home, where I started following the book the very next morning. It had exercises and menus laid out in the book. Mother always asked what we wanted to eat at our evening meal. I started telling her what I would like each night for supper and she would buy it. I couldn't pick the meal at school so sometimes I would take my lunch. I always had to fix my own breakfast, since we no longer had a maid, so that part was easy. At school, instead of being uninterested in the sports at PE, I began to really take part. I always walked home from school, but started walking faster, instead of just sauntering along. By the time I was 14, I was 110 pounds and 5'6". (By the time I was a Senior I was 5"8" and the 110 pounds was a little too thin for my height.)

Aunt Ann came to visit one week to check on my weight program and see how I was doing. She said to Mother, "For God's sake Ava, why don't you buy that girl a bra?" Mother said, "I had never noticed that she needed one." Aunt Ann told her that I not only needed a bra, but needed to know about how my body was changing. She asked mother if she had told me about periods and she said, "No". Aunt Ann looked at me and said, "I will tell her if you don't." She turned to look at Mother. Her face was red and she said, "Fine" as she walked out of the room. I listened in shock about what she was telling me, because no one I ran with, including my best friend, Edith had ever mentioned it. Edith had an older sister so I assumed she knew all about it, but was too embarrassed to share this with me.

Now I knew, and had 3 bras which I was not fond of wearing. All this was overwhelming. Aunt Ann did not venture into boys and reproduction. Maybe the shocked look on my face from the previous information was more than she could handle. Fortunately, that was the same year I quit playing with the boys and found girlfriends and started asking questions. There was very limited sex education in the school system as they left that job to the family.

There were other things that complicate the teen years and I was just about to experience one of those. On Easter that year, I had a surprise I never would have expected. I had always attended the Methodist Church and became a member when I was 11. Mother had only stepped into that church one time and it was to see my conversion. Two weeks before Easter, Mother told me that she was going to go to church with me for the Easter service. I was shocked as she had never attended church since she was a child. I said "Okay, that would be nice." I did not know until the following week that several of the mothers were going to be attending dressed the same as their daughter. I found that out when a large box arrived from Sears and Roebuck mail order. Mother said, "Come see what I bought for us." As I looked at the garments being removed from the box, I was speechless. There were two navy dresses with large pink polka dots and 2 white lacy blouses. 2 identical pale pink small hats matched the dresses. They had crinolines made into the dress to help make it look "fluffy." I said "What are these for? She said "I heard that your church is having a competition to pick out the mother and daughter who look the most alike. I thought we would compete. I will fix your hair and mine exactly alike and we'll wear these cute little hats with our dresses. "I heard myself say okay." I felt "goofy" as I hated polka dots and was embarrassed to be dressed like her, when most of the competition turned out to be girls from age 4 to 12. Somehow, I thought to myself, "I will make it through the next 5 years in spite of mother."

CHAPTER 9

SEX EDUCATION FOR ADULTS

Apparently, there must have been very little sex education for adults, also. When all this talking about sex started, I remembered that when I was about 6 years old, a neighboring town had a sex education film about intercourse and birth control for adults. They featured it for 2 or 3 nights. They would run it two times a night because they allowed only men to the first feature then only women to the second feature. I knew that, because my parents took me with them to attend. I stayed with Mother while Daddy attended, then stayed with Daddy while Mother took part.

They called the men in, and I just stood around, while Mother visited with the other women waiting. As usual, she was not concerned about my whereabouts, so I snuck around the corner to read the marquee. It said, "Sexual Education for Men and Women," then listed the times. Mother didn't care that I saw it or didn't think I would know what it meant. She was right.

When it came Mother's time to attend, Daddy stood on the same corner to wait. On that corner was a nice jewelry store, and he was looking in the window. I could barely tiptoe high enough to see what was in the window. I walked on my tiptoes to the end where the corner was and "lo and behold" I found one of the first Mickey Mouse watches. I drug Daddy down to see it and told him how much I would love to have it, and it could be for Christmas. I begged and nagged for a time, so he finally gave in to go look at it. It had a bright red patent leather band, and Mickey's yellow gloves were the hands that showed the time. I hugged Daddy's leg and asked him if I could try it on. He said "Yes." I put the coveted piece on my little skinny wrist. It was obvious that we would have to poke another hole to make it fit properly. I looked up to see my Daddy paying for the watch. I said "Can I wear it?" and he said, "yes". I didn't care that it didn't fit. I wore it anyway.

When Mother came out of the show, she was not happy about the watch. First, she said it was too expensive and second, if it was going to be a Christmas present it needed to go back in the box. She also told Daddy that he was spoiling me and that I would turn out to be worthless, if he continued to let me have anything I wanted. To make her happy and keep her from fussing at Daddy, I put it back in the box without saying a word. I still have that watch, and have never been told I was worthless, yet.

On the way home that night Daddy asked her if she learned anything new at the movie. She said it was embarrassing and she would talk about it later. He said he had learned some new things that he had never heard of before about women. I was listening and wondering what new things he was talking about. I said, "I wish I could have gone to the show. Did they have Mickey Mouse cartoons?" They both laughed and Daddy said, "No". I said "It must have been boring." Daddy said, "I only went to the one that the men attended. You need to ask your mother what her show was about and if it was boring." Mother said, "I do not want to talk about this movie, it was only for grown-ups and when Lydia grows up, she can watch it. This conversation is over." She glared at him like she did when she was angry with him, so I didn't dare say another word.

I guess the time never came for Mother to tell me about sex. The movie never came to town again that I remember. Now I am 13 and no wiser about anything, but my own body changes. So, I started quizzing my best friend who was from a large family and had older siblings. I also visited with another girl who had all brothers to find out what boys were experiencing on their way to puberty. She wasn't much help.

CHAPTER 10

THE CONDOM CONUNDRUM

One day I went into my parent's room to search for something Mother had asked me to get. She had told me it was in the bottom drawer, but I was reading a comic book, and not paying full attention. I opened the top drawer and on the left was a loaded gun which Daddy used to keep in the closet. To the right was a box containing little flat, white round boxes. I took the top off one of the boxes to look, and it had what appeared to be a white balloon in it. On the box it had resided in was a piece of paper explaining how to put this thing they were calling a "condom" on your penis. Then it mentioned on the box that it was the best protection for men. I wanted to know more about why this penis needed to be "protected."

I decided the friend who had all brothers would be the best to ask about what a penis was. I asked her and she told me what it was and described what it looked like. With this piece of information, I contemplated what purpose this condom had in a male's life. I forgot to ask her why a penis needed protecting. The only thing I could come up with recalling my "vast" knowledge of sex and women's periods, was the possibility that men also had periods. This made sense to me because why else would a man need something to enclose his penis with unless he had to catch something besides pee coming out of it. That purpose would have protected the penis from spilling the blood all over their under-wear. The pads the women were wearing didn't seem like they would control a male problem since there was no way to capture the fluid coming out in a pad when he was shaped so differently than a female.

I didn't want to ask any more about it until I stayed again with Aunt Ann as she didn't seem to be upset about the sexual subjects. When I told her the condom story she laughed. Then she apologized for laughing when she saw my serious face. She said, "Has anyone ever told you where babies come from?" I said, "No, but I know that they grow in women's stomachs." She said, "I have some books that you need to read so that you may be more knowledgeable about all the things involving sex." I took those books to my bedroom that night and read them from cover to cover.

Now, armed with all this new information, and nearly 14, I was ready to enter the world of puberty. All my friends had started having periods and that was the topic of the day when I was around other girls. Some of the girls had begun to look at me as an oddity because I had no periods yet. When I was almost 15, I had assessed the problem and come to the conclusion that I knew what was wrong. Possibly the reason that I had never "start-ed," was I was going to be a boy!

I wasn't really happy about this problem, but I had played with boys a large part of my life, and decided I could live with it if I had no choice. I was a little concerned about the bras if this was going to be my true fate. Right before my 15th birthday, I started! My Mother, as usual, was not at home and I did not want to tell Daddy. So, I sat down and waited until she returned home. When I told her, she acted shocked, so I wondered if she thought I was an oddity, too. She got me all the necessary supplies and I entered a new life as a real female, just like all my friends.

CHAPTER 11

HALLOWEEN BOX SUPPER

At 13, I was beginning to notice that some older boys were quite attractive. I had never paid any attention to them before, although I had a crush on a boy in grade school. I used to have my mother drive me by both theaters when the Saturday matinees played to see which line he was standing in. I was about 10 or 11 years old. I would go into the movie, where he would sit by me and hold my hand so no one else could see. As the years went by, he became a really wonderful friend, and as a teenager I did not date him, but have always loved him like a brother.

Now that I was 13, I really took notice of men's looks. Right before Halloween that year, a school in the county had what was known as a Box Supper. This was a fund raiser where all the mothers of the children in the school as well as any other females who wanted to participate, would take a shoe box and decorate it in autumn colors. Inside the box, they would place food items for two people, an entrée of some sort with a vegetable along with a dessert and bread. Others might make sandwiches or some other favorite for their male counterpart. The girls would put their name on the bottom of the box and an auctioneer would auction each box. Some of the men were spouses of the box maker thus they knew what their wife's boxes contained so they would bid on it until they won. There were a lot of young people who would bid on their girlfriend's box so they might eat together.

Mother and I both had a box. My box looked very similar to another box sitting on the table. When it came to bid my box, a very handsome man in his 20's bid on it. 50 cents was the bid and someone else said 75 cents. The young man said a dollar. The auctioneer asked if that was the final bid, and I was surprised but excited to eat with someone so handsome, who had bid so much on my box. What I did not know is that he was in love with one of the new teachers, and her box was almost exactly like mine. Then, someone else bid on my box and the young man raised his bid again. After doing this twice, he bought my box. He was so handsome that I could hardly take my eyes off of him! They looked at the bottom of the box and called my name. I was elated! His eyes showed the shock of what he had done. He turned around to look at his girlfriend and she had her hand over her mouth, and did not look very happy.

Three boxes later, the other box like mine came up, and the young man bid again. An old farmer in overalls had bid first and offered 25 cents. The young man bid 50 cents, then the old farmer said a dollar. It must have been more money than the young man had, so the old farmer got the bid. When they called her name, I then realized what had happened but the young man already knew. He looked so sad, and as much as I wanted to eat and look at his handsome face, I said, "I think you bought the wrong box. Would you like to have her come eat with you out of my box, and I will eat her box with the old gentleman?" His face lit up and he said he would ask her, and the man that bought the box, if they would mind doing that. The man that bought the box said he would, if he could see the contents of both boxes first. After looking he decided he would keep the box he had. I told him I would eat with him instead of the teacher, and he said, "No, I want the lady that came with the box."

So, I sat down and shared my meal with the handsome man who never told me his name. We had very little conversation and the girlfriend looked so sad she was not eating, while the old man was busy eating the contents. He seemed to have no concern about what had transpired. I'm sure that the contents of her box were much more exciting than mine, since she had planned hers for the man she was in love with. As a footnote, they did end up getting married and living happily ever after. He never did get ugly as he aged, plus missing that one meal probably didn't harm their relationship.

CHAPTER 12

UNEXPECTED SEX EDUCATION

Later that year, I still had never seen a naked male. But one day after going to a friend's house, my mother called and said she was on her way to pick me up. My friend's mother said I could sit on the back steps while I waited for her. She was planning to mop the floor, and her daughter was going to have to dust the furniture. I gathered my things up and sat down on the highest step to wait.

The road my mother would come down was to my left, and there was a large row of shrubs separating the next- door neighbor's yard from the driveway in front of me. As usual Mother was late, so I was bored and was looking down the shrub line, when I saw a teenage boy standing facing me. His pants were unzipped, and he backed up between the last two shrubs. He was smiling and pulling something out of his pants. I saw that he was holding something in his hand. All of sudden he started shaking it, and I realized that what he was shaking was his penis. I turned my head to the left so I would not have to look at him because I was so embarrassed, but my curiosity to see what a penis looked like overcame me. My head was looking straight ahead but my eyes were to the right so as not to miss my chance to see a real penis.

About that time, some liquid came out of it, and I thought he needs a condom so that mess wouldn't have happened. (I still wasn't aware of the real purpose for a condom.) I never had another thought about the problem, because mother pulled in the drive, as I got up to get in the car. The boy was still standing there, and mother saw him the minute I opened the door. She said, "Get in the car and don't look back, there's a nasty boy shaking his thing at us, over in the shrubbery."

I couldn't think of what to say to that. I didn't know if I should tell her that the "thing" was a penis. So instead, I finally said, "Where?" She started on a tirade of how awful it was to do that in front of women and how sick he must be. All the time, I was dying to ask her if she knew the name of that thing he was shaking at us? I couldn't do it without laughing, so I let it go. But that day I knew what it looked like, and now I thought I knew what the condom was for, but I was wrong.

CHAPTER 13

EXPERIMENTING WITH CONDOMS

I shared this story with a girl friend of mine, named Susan, who had a great sense of humor. We laughed and she told me that she had found some condoms at her house. She had asked a male cousin of hers about how they were used. She shared this information with me. Now, I had finally found out that birth control was the purpose of the condom, not periods or catching liquids that flowed out of it. I felt as if I knew it all.

Susan's cousin had told her that he had read in an advertisement that condoms were so strong that they could hold up to 1 to 2 gallons of water. We thought that would make a good experiment, even though it was not the kind you could take to your biology class for a grade. She told him we were going to try the water trick and would report back to him. He said he bet we didn't have the nerve to do it. Oh, yeah!

Susan came to spend the night that weekend. I stole a condom out of Daddy's supply, while mother was gone, and Daddy was in the living room engrossed in his favorite tv show. We locked ourselves in our only bathroom at the end of the hall. We had taken a measuring cup to get the appropriate amount plus paper and pen to write it down. I was holding the condom in the lavatory. To be able to pour the water without spilling it in the floor. Susan was pouring the water out of the faucet into the cup to measure the amount. I was transferring the water into the opening. At around 6 cups of water, it became hard to manage to get the water out of the faucet because the condom was filling up the bowl. We put 2 more cups in, when we realized, we were going to have to transport the water filled condom to the bathtub. Susan and I picked it up, while I was holding the top twisted and proceeded to move it 5 feet to the tub. About a foot away from the tub, the water began to shift and we began to move around trying not to lose control of it. We looked as though we were dancing on an icy floor. All of a sudden, we lost total control as it slipped out of our wet hands, fell onto the floor, bursting and throwing water every direction. We both yelled which brought Daddy to the bathroom door. "What are you girls doing?" he said. I said, "Just taking turns styling our hair." I could see the water easing its way under the bathroom door. I knew if the water made it to his side of the door, he would ask us to open up.

Thank goodness he turned and went back to the living room to continue with his TV program just as the water oozed its way under the door. I peeked out and saw he was gone, I immediately ran to my bedroom and grabbed a chenille bedspread, which we threw in the floor to soak up the water. Then I climbed through the bathroom window carrying the bedspread, waited until my eyes adjusted to the dark, then hung it on the clothesline to dry. I could not take it out the back door because Daddy could see me from the living room. I had sneaked out of the house to take the bedspread, and now I had to sneak back in. The bathroom window was too high so I had to climb into the bedroom. When I walked into the bathroom, Susan said "We've got another problem. I tried to flush the condom down the toilet and it won't flush." We tried the second time. I don't know what caused it to keep floating back up. Perhaps we did not have enough water pressure to pull it down. We dug it out of the toilet and I sneaked out the second time. I got a shovel and dug a hole behind the henhouse to bury it. There was very little light so I was hoping that it was not visible. I had to check it the next morning before daylight in case somebody came out to gather eggs. I almost forgot to bring in the chenille bedspread. We did not get much rest that night between the giggling and laughing about the experiment until midnight, and having to get up so early to hide what we had done. We put it all down in my diary as a failed experiment.

Susan and I decided to tell her cousin to experiment with the water volume the condom would hold. He never did. Guess he didn't have the nerve to do it.

CHAPTER 14

DIRTY DANCING

A few months later, there was a dance class for girls that was scheduled to meet once a month to teach ballroom dancing. All my friends had signed up, so I decided I would too. The teacher had some older boys from high school who were also students to dance with us. At the conclusion of each song, everyone would change partners to learn the next few steps. I looked at the boys standing there waiting for their first partner, and there was a handsome boy that looked familiar. All of the girls were looking at him. He had black wavy hair, beautiful eyes and long lashes. The girls were probably thinking they hoped he picked them. All of a sudden, I realized that was the boy in the shrubs! I had not seen him up close nor studied his face when he exposed himself. I was too busy trying to see what he was shaking at me.

He started walking toward me. I certainly did not want to have him as a dance partner so I turned toward another boy. He was an older brother, of one of my friends. I said, "May I be your partner?" He said "Yes." The "shrub boy" turned to a pretty blond girl that I did not know and asked her. I could tell by the way she smiled and tilted her head that she was excited to be his partner. The first dance was a waltz and when we started, I noticed that the "shrub boy" was holding his partner right up against him. The teacher stopped and instructed the boys to back away from the girls and position their arm around their waist, holding them about six inches away from them. We started again and everything seemed to be going as planned. We traded off to the next partner and started another song. The" shrub boy" pulled that girl tight to him and was dancing with his back to the teacher. Once more she admonished him about the perfect distance and he loosened up his grip then moved away.

This went on every time he changed partners. I could see the teacher was getting frustrated and all the boys thought it was funny. None of the girls wanted to be his partner after witnessing how he refused to keep the distance the teacher had requested. We took a break and then when we came back to the dance floor, he walked right over and grabbed me by the arm. The teacher put us in position for a two-step and the first time he had his back to the teacher he yanked me up close to him. I did not know what an erection was, as it had never been part of my sketchy sex education. But I found out that day! I pulled myself away from him and told the teacher that I was going to have to go home. She asked, "Why?" I could have lied and said I didn't feel good but I was always outspoken, so I told her I did not want to dance with him. She suggested I dance with someone else. Now the girls all said they weren't dancing with him either.

The teacher knew what the problem was, but I couldn't decide if she was afraid of losing the dance lesson money or some other reason. I later learned that this boy had recently moved to town because he was experiencing sexual problems in another town. His parents had difficulty keeping him in school because of exposing himself and making sexual gestures toward female students. I was afraid of him. Especially since he had exposed himself in the bushes and didn't seem to worry about minding the teacher. I didn't want him to know my name or where I lived.

I did not go back to the class, but I told my mother and for one time, she agreed with me. She said it would be best for me to drop the dance class in order to avoid him. Since she had seen him when I did, exposing himself, she was more sympathetic than usual. A few weeks later, he attempted to rape a girl. She was sunbathing in her back yard out of view, unless you were in her yard. Apparently, he had been watching her for some time. Her dad caught him and they took him to jail. He did not come back to our school, and I often wondered where he ended up.

CHAPTER 15

STRANGE BOY PROBLEMS

That fall when I turned 13 and entered the 8th grade, a new boy came to school. He entered the 8th grade, but he was 19 years old. The purpose of attending school for him was to finish eighth grade so he might enter military service. He wasn't much bigger than anyone else in our classes. He had a round face, with cheeks that looked as though he had the mumps. It reminded me of a squirrel with an acorn in each jaw. He had moved two doors down from my parent's business. His father was very elderly and his mother was about 45. He also had a sister. They had goats in their back yard that they milked, and this provided them with cheese and milk. He had bunnies in a hutch, that they killed for the meat, as well as chickens in their backyard which they kept for meat and eggs.

From the first day he entered the 8th grade class room for Math, he began to flirt with me. I had no interest in him, but he sat right beside me and would not leave me alone. Sometimes he was so annoying that I would kick him in the shins. He acted like he loved being kicked so I soon quit and tried to ignore him again. After school, he would come to our house and visit my parents, so I would go to my room. In the summer when I had to pick berries of all kinds in our garden as one of my chores, he would show up and start picking with the pretense of helping me. He knew that my parents were at work, and I was alone. Then as he picked, he would get closer and closer to me. One time he said to me "Is that a bra you have on?" I didn't answer, so he said, "Let me feel and see if you have anything to go in it." I slapped him across the face making one of his puffy cheeks, redder. I jumped up and went in the house and locked the doors. That day, I put him in the same "class" as the "shrub boy." He still continued to harass me at school. He would write me love letters and leave them in my desk. They never had a capital "I", plus he never used a period at the end of a sentence. Therefore, you never knew where these run on sentences started or stopped.

If I went anywhere with friends at night, when I came home, he would be sitting in the living room with my father watching TV. When I had a date, he would show up at the time I was leaving and would stay in the living room until I returned that evening. I would tell Daddy goodnight and go directly to my room. He would then leave. I never figured out how he knew that I had a date or the time they would be there. I wondered if he sat across the road and waited until someone pulled in our drive to get me. I complained to my dad, but he and my mother felt sorry for him and never did anything about him hanging around all the time.

He was smothering me to death with his constant presence. He did not have a car, but he walked everywhere that he knew I was going to be. The term "stalker" was not in use yet and my parents thought his attention to me was funny, until Daddy caught him one night outside our bathroom peeping into the window while I was taking a bath. Daddy had stepped outside with a gun so he was lucky to still be alive. He told him not to come back in our yard, and he didn't for a year or so. Instead, he started giving all of his attention to another girl who had just moved to town. What a relief! Apparently, she didn't mind and I was happy for both of them.

At the end of that 8th year of schooling, he applied for the Navy. They turned him down because he had not finished high school, or that is what he told everyone. Someone else said he probably could not pass the test to join. Shortly after that he applied for the Army and was accepted. When he finally made it into the military and was stationed out of the country, he wrote my mother and asked for a picture of me. She sent it to him without asking me. He told all the men he was stationed with that I was his girlfriend and produced the picture as proof. He asked my mother to write him, and he would send her gifts addressed to me. When he received letters from mother, he said they were letters from me. When I found out what he was doing from one of his relatives, I confronted Mother and asked her to quit writing him. I also asked her to quit sending any more pictures of me to him. She finally did. I do know he stayed in the military for 4 years but did not re-enlist, but from that point on, I never heard from him. I can't say I was sorry.

CHAPTER 16

BECOMING "STREET SAVVY"

The summer, when I turned 14, a girl a year younger than me, went out with a bunch of boys in town, and they all took their turn with her. This resulted in the boys all having to have shots for some sexual disease they acquired. I had heard about it and heard the terminology "gang bang" for the first time. I didn't give any thought to this having anything to do with me or my girl-friends. This resulted in a lecture, by my daddy about never getting in a car with more than one boy in it. Very few boys I knew had driver's license yet, so I listened but most of it drifted out my other ear. If I had known what could happen, I would have listened intently. This turned out to be a very worthwhile lecture, later.

Since the incident had happened a few of the rougher boys in town had decided that there must be other girls interested in doing the same thing with them. There were groups of guys who would ride around whistling and flirting with girls walking home from school. They were usually girls in groups and it was daylight, so it was not too much of a danger.

A few weeks later, I had been on a school bus trip out of town and we all arrived back at school a little after dark. Like Mother had done so many times before, she was late in coming after me. The bus left, and I was alone with a lady teacher who had accompanied us on the trip. 20 minutes after we had arrived, everyone had been picked up but me. My house was less than a ½ mile from the school which was well lit and across the street was a drive- in restaurant along with a service station, both with bright lighting. I finally said to the teacher, "I live straight down this road, so I will walk home, so you can go home." She asked if I was sure? I pointed and said, "I live right across from the City Limit sign. I'll be fine." Looking back, I wondered why she didn't volunteer to take me home. I suppose Mother had been late so many times, perhaps she thought if she took me home, we would expect it every time. She drove off, and I crossed the road to started walking home in the light. Once I had gone the first block, there was no light of any kind. I knew my way and could easily be home in a matter of a few minutes.

I was walking as close to the buildings as I could so as not the be noticed. About that time a car passed by me with the windows down, and I could hear male voices cussing and laughing. They were cruising to the end of City Limits where everyone made a U-turn and started to cruise back across town, looking for action. Most of the cars were at the drive-ins and hangouts for teens on that street. The U-turn was across the street from our home. The car made the turn when I was almost to my parent's business. As it made the turn, the lights shined on me and the car pulled in our drive. They were whistling and yelling at me.

It was four boys who had a so-so reputation in town. The one driving and his brother were the only two I knew. One was about my age and the other was just old enough to drive. The driver started calling my name and moving up right beside me. I picked up my walking pace, but he had me trapped between the car and the building I was passing.

He said, "Where you going?" I said, "Home". He said, "All the action is in town, why don't you go with us and we'll have a big time". My mind was working overtime trying to figure out how I was going to get out of this dilemma. I heard one of the boys from the back seat say, "Let me out I'll help her in the car." When he leaned forward, I recognized him and he did not have a good reputation. Truly, he was someone to be afraid of! I knew I was outnumbered and had to come up with something right now! I said a silent prayer for help.

That's when I made my decision. I stopped dead in my tracks. His car came to a stop beside me. I leaned over toward the driver. I put my hand on his arm and rubbed my fingers back and forth. Then I leaned in close to his face and whispered in his ear. I said, "I've always liked you ever since we used to ride horses together, when we were little. I could get in the car with just you, and just the two of us could go back to town. Why don't you take them back to the drive-in and drop them off? Then I'll wait for you to come back and get me." He thought for a second or two and said, "I'll be right back." I could hear the other boys complaining as they were pulling onto the highway, but he was driving as fast as he could, headed to drop them off. It worked, but after praying for help I felt badly about lying.

I stood there waving. I waited for a few minutes to make sure he couldn't see me in the darkness. Then I started running as fast as I could! The drive in was across the street from the high school where I had started from, so he didn't have far to go. I kept looking back to see if he was coming, then I saw the lights coming back my way, right before I got to the City Limits sign! There was a piece of equipment blocking his view of me so I jumped the first ditch across the county road. I looked back and saw that he had pulled in to where I said I would wait. I could hear him yelling, "Lydia" over and over. I then jumped the second ditch and threw myself over the fence around our yard. He threw gravel driving out of the parking lot where he had left me. He was furious and his windows were down, so I could hear all of the abusive language he was saying about me. He was

65

headed toward me. I was laying in the flower beds as he came across the street from our house to make the U-turn. He shined his lights on our yard, but could not see me for the flowers. He sat there for a while with his bright lights on. My heart was beating fast from the run and I was breathing hard. I was afraid he'd get out of the car to look and could hear me breathing. Then, I heard him cussing, and he squealed his tires when he pulled back onto the highway, to go back toward town.

When I was sure he was gone, I got up to go into the house. I looked at the clock and Mother had not come home yet. I yelled at Daddy who was watching TV and told him I was home. I then told him I was going to get ready for bed and do some homework, as I did not want him to see me with my clothes all dirty. A few minutes later when Mother finally came in, she opened the door to my bedroom and said she had been looking for me and why didn't I wait? She then asked me how I got the grass stains on my clothes. I told her the story and she was shocked. But as usual, she said it couldn't have been as bad as I said it was. I said, "How do you know? You weren't there! When have you ever been there when I needed you?"

The next thing out of her mouth was, "Lower your voice, don't tell your Daddy, you know how he is and he would hurt those boys or worse." She did not share this scary problem with my Daddy ever, nor did I. She told me not to leave the school again until she came to pick me up. I told her that I would stay at the school, but I wanted her to arrive on time. I told her from now on if she didn't arrive on time, I would have the school call Daddy to come get me. This made her mad and she walked off in a "huff," but she showed up on time to get me from then on until I was old enough to drive.

CHAPTER 17

MAKING THE CHANGE TO FEMINISM

While I was still 14 my Daddy and I had put out jugs for "jug fishing" on the island, where daddy had grown up. We had put the jugs in place the day before. Because I would get muddy and wet, my clothes were old jeans plus a tattered shirt. My shoes I wore had obviously been wet many times before, as the toes reached up toward the sun enough to be uncomfortable, if I had to walk very far. My hair had not been combed nor my face washed. I got out of bed, put on my fishing clothes and climbed into the Jeep.

It was a beautiful day with the sun peeking through the cypress trees, the air smelled so good from the wildflowers. The water was crystal clear in places that hadn't been stirred up by the elusive species of fish along the edges of the bayou. Occasionally, you would see small animals and birds searching for food in the trees and on the ground. The island was like a step back in time. The forests were so thick and the ground cover so perfect for game. I have always loved it and understood what my grandfather saw in this neck of the woods when he purchased it in 1899.

Daddy wanted to be at the island early to pull the jugs out

before the predator fish like the "Gar" started eating them. (A Garfish is a long slender fish that can grow to be 20-30 inches in length. Their jaws are elongated and have teeth that look like needles. Their fins are on the back of their body. They resemble an eel but are light in color. The first time you see one it is a frightening experience as they will remind you of a prehistoric creature.) I refuse to try and take a hook out of their mouth because of those horrible teeth. I have upset Daddy before by taking a knife, then cutting the line, leaving the hook in its mouth. Daddy was very frugal and would pout over the loss of the hook. Fortunately, there were no gars caught today. We completed the release of the brim and catfish from all the jugs, placed them into a live well and re-baited the hooks. We then loaded the catch into the Jeep and started home.

It was mid-morning, and Daddy had stopped by the implement business to see Mother before taking me home. When we walked into the building, there was one of the farmers at the parts counter talking to Mother. Daddy and I said hello then Mother said, "Jim has something he wants to talk to us about. It involves Lydia."

My heart was in my throat, and my mind was rushing, trying to think of what I might have done to cause this farmer to be looking for me. He turned to Daddy and said, "You know that the town has built a new swimming pool, and they are having an opening celebration in two weeks. They decided to have a swimsuit beauty competition during the opening. I coach a Babe Ruth league called the Cardinals, and we want to sponsor a girl. The team voted that they would like Lydia to be our representative. Would the 3 of you approve of that?"

No one spoke but Mother who said, "I don't think Lydia would be interested. Just look at her, she is too much of a "tomboy" and far too modest to parade around in front of a bunch of people in a swimsuit. I can't imagine why anyone would pick her when there are so many pretty young ladies in town. My opinion is that you should select one that is well groomed and feminine. That type of girl would probably win the contest for your team. Lydia is not feminine at all, nor does she appear to want to be at this time of her life."

I think my feelings were hurt. I couldn't say because I had never felt all the emotions before that were running through my mind, because of what she said. It was true that I was extremely modest, but I think that comes of being an only child and never having shared any intimacies with other siblings. The part about being picked by the boys did not surprise me as some of them had been my playmates since I was little. I had never thought about my femininity, but I never got a chance to open my mouth because Daddy spoke up.

Daddy said to Mother," This is not our choice, this is Lydias. This is an honor, and if she wants to participate it will be up to her." Mother glared at Daddy and said, "You're just going to let her make a fool of herself in front of the town. She will be embarrassed and so will we." I was looking down at my feet with the curled toes of my shoes looking back at me. I was thinking that Mother had already caused our family enough embarrassment in front of the town for all of us. A little more couldn't hurt. I looked at Mr. Jim whom I could see was very uncomfortable about this situation.

Before either of my parents said another word, I turned to the farmer and said, "Mr. Jim, I would like to do it." Daddy said, "What she means is she will be proud to represent your team." Mother's face turned "beet red" and she said, "She's on her own, I'm not helping with this" and stalked out of the room! Jim seemed relieved, then he hurriedly said thank you to Daddy and me, then left. Daddy looked at me, laughed, then said, "I guess you're going to have to comb your hair and wash your face." I said "I'll call Aunt Ann to help me" and hugged my Daddy's neck. (Aunt Ann was my mother's only sister and who I thought of as my second "Mother,")

Mother was in a sulk for the rest of the day. I heard her tell Daddy that I didn't know anything about make-up, because I only had a beginner's tube of lipstick, which I rarely wore. (There was a lipstick sold that all teenagers wore that looked like it was yellow-orange in the tube. When applied to the lips it turned different colors on different people.) That was the extent of the make-up most girls my age wore. My hair still had a lot of natural curl and was a golden blond, but I did not know how to style it. I had never worn high heel shoes and hated the idea of shaving my legs. The worse problem was I did not have a swimming suit other than a baggy looking pink and white, checked one piece that I had swam in a few times. The white part of the suit had become sort of brown. My dad had taken me to the chute right off the island, to teach me to swim in the muddy river which had badly discolored the swimsuit.

I told Daddy I would need money for a swimsuit and shoes. I would talk to Aunt Ann about makeup and how to walk in heels. Aunt Ann agreed to help me. She was so excited that I had been selected! Even though Mother was displeased, she always let her older sister have her way. Besides, Mother had already said she wanted nothing to do with the contest, so I wasn't about to ask her for help. Money in hand, that Daddy had given me, Aunt Ann and I went to a store in a neighboring town that carried swimsuits. After trying on several, we decided on a red one- piece suit with a round neck trimmed in navy and white. My shoes were 3" red sandals with a navy bow across the front. I tried them on and could not walk in them, but I was determined to learn.

I went home with only 10 days to learn to walk in the shoes. Aunt Ann took me to the beauty shop and had my hair trimmed and we started practicing with make-up. Aunt Ann gave me a book that told how to have perfect posture while walking like the models on tv did. You were to place the book on your head and walk with one foot in front of the other to look graceful. It said to let your hands hang loosely at your side so as not to appear stiff and uncomfortable. This was the hardest part. I was 5'6" at the time and only weighed 110 pounds thanks to the diet Aunt Ann had helped me with last year. With the shoes I was 5'9" tall. When I finally practiced for the last time and looked at myself in the mirror, I could at least say I would not fall down, but remembering to smile at the same time was difficult. I was determined to do my best in this contest after Mother had said I wasn't capable.

Since Daddy wouldn't go to town ever, I knew he wasn't going to take me to the contest. Mother told Aunt Ann she was going to go with her. Mother had always gone to everything I was in since I was a small child. I have said before that she always wanted to present a good mother image to the town. This was another opportunity even though Mr. Jim and his baseball team knew better. Aunt Ann had brought Uncle Billy, and after doing my makeup, she told Mother she was ready to go. Mother decided at the last minute to take me in her car. I thought she was probably wanting to be there to tell me, "I told you so" if I didn't do well.

When we arrived at the new swimming pool, I had on my clothes and a pair of sandals. When I saw the large amount of cars parked there, I began to get nervous. Mr. Jim and his ball team were there, and all the observers were lined up against the fence. Mother said, "Are you sure you want to do this in front of all these people?" I said nothing. "Are you going to get out or do you want to go home?" she said. I said "I'll go in." I stepped out of the car and walked slowly across the parking lot to the pool dressing room carrying my suit and shoes. There were 12 girls of all ages (14-18) participating that were already dressed, putting on their makeup and doing their hair. I went into the dressing room and put on my suit and the high heels. I stepped out and looked at myself in the mirror and acted as though I was looking at my makeup and hair. I was really just afraid to touch my face and hair, because I did not know how to fix either feature. I also was trying to make my face relax and smile.

About that time, a lady came into the room with cards with numbers on them. She turned them upside down and fanned them out. She told us that this would be our number in the contest. We were asked to draw a card to select what number each of us would be. She said to hold the cards on the right side of our hip. If we did that, the judges would be able to see our number as we passed by. She explained we would file out of the room, walk along the fence, stop in front of the judges, then turn around slowly so they could see you from all sides, walk along the fence to the back, stop next to the building and wait there until all the other numbers are called. I listened intently, then thought I will watch the other girls and do what they do. Big shock when I turned over my card and discovered that I was number one! Now I was afraid! Too late, she was pinning the banner that said Cardinals on my shoulder, and I remembered why I was there. The older girls had all been in contests that I attended with my friends. They were experienced, while 3 other girls and myself were not. The Cardinals had faith in me, and I was going to try to do my best for them.

I tried to remember the rules of what to do and kept turning them over in my mind. When I heard the loud speaker call, "Contestant #1" I hesitated for a few seconds until the girl behind me said, "It's your turn to go." I thought about what the book said about standing up straight like you had a puppet string holding your head up, then let your arms loosen up and put your left foot forward and step out with your right. Repeat! I was moving, but I had forgotten to smile. My mouth was so dry, my lips were stuck to my teeth! I ran my tongue between my teeth and gums and forced my mouth into a smile. I heard some people applauding and yelling Lydia. That's when I realized the team was hanging on the fence. I relaxed a little and the smile became more natural.

A flash crossed my mind as I walked! How grateful I was that I had worn braces which had been taken off a couple of years ago. I had one front tooth that went forward while one went back. When I closed my mouth, the forward tooth pushed into my lip making it look like I had a lump in my lip. The braces had brought both teeth under control. My Dad had insisted on my having them because he said "You look like you could eat a pumpkin through a picket fence, and we need to do something about that now." We had to drive 300 miles round trip each time I went to the nearest orthodontist. I shuddered to think I could not have opened my mouth to smile without that correction.

As I turned to go toward the judges, I could feel my heart pounding in my head. I slowed my walk and stopped in front of the area where the judges were seated. I made my slow turn. (This was my major concern as I never felt secure in the heels as I turned around.) I was smiling all the way around. I stepped away and fought the desire to run toward the end of the building! I managed to keep the steps slow enough to not look too panicked. When I reached the building and turned to face the onlookers, the relief was probably evident in my face, but by that time, number 2 had been called. Everyone was now focused on her.

After all the girls had done their march, they asked us all to come line up in front of the judges. They said only 3 would be selected, the queen along with two runner ups. We then returned to the pool dressing room while the judges, who were from another state were introduced. They then reviewed the contestant information and made a selection. In my mind, I had already picked the winner who was the older sister of a friend of mine. She had so much personality and was very popular in school. I had watched her walk with such confidence and grace that I knew she was the one. She also was a very pretty girl.

It was time to announce the winner and everyone was nervous. The 2nd runner up was called which was one of the 14-year -olds in my class at school. The first runner up was called and again it was another 14- year- old from school. When they called the winner, I thought I was dreaming when I hear them say the queen of the new swimming pool is #1, Lydia Constantine. Again, one of the girls behind me said, "They're calling your name, you need to go." I was in a daze! I don't know how gracefully I walked up to join the two other girls. They then placed the paper crown on my head. I was so excited that a jeweled crown could not have been better! I could see Aunt Ann and Uncle Billy smiling and clapping. Mother was clapping too, but not as excitedly as they were.

Jim and his ball team were excited! The boys were whistling and yelling. I was more pleased that I hadn't let them down than I was that I had won. Mr. Jim and the boys came over. He said he wanted to thank me for representing them. I told him I was proud to be their queen candidate and felt honored that I had been asked to participate. After lots of congratulatory well-wishers had visited with me, I got into the car with mother to start home.

All of a sudden, I remembered the couple who owned the drugstore where all the teenagers hung out. They had helped Mother by babysitting me when Daddy was hospitalized so long during grade school. They had asked that I come by after the contest to tell them the results. They wanted to know how I had done.

As Mother and I left to go home, I suddenly recalled that I had told the couple I would come by. I asked Mother to take me to their store for a minute, and she said, you still have on your swimsuit, we're going home. I said, "No, I promised." She turned around and I walked into their store and announced, "I know who won." and I had my crown behind me. When I showed them the crown, they were so excited for me. They both gave me a big hug. We then headed for home. I jumped out of the car and ran into the living room where Daddy was watching TV and yelled, "Guess who won?" and he said, "I don't know but I know who should have won." I put the crown on him and told him I was the winner and he hugged me and said, "You'll always be the winner for me!" That was a happy day for me and it must have been the ego boost I needed to become more feminine. I started looking in the mirror while caring more about my hair, face and how I was dressed.

CHAPTER 18

BUYING THE FAMILY ISLAND FARM

My grandfather, Calvin Constantine still owned the farm on the island he had purchased in 1899. He raised his family there after their move from across the river. He had decided to sell the farm instead of keeping it for his children to inherit. He told them all about his plans and how much he wanted for it. He said he was offering it to any of the family that would want to purchase it. If none of the children wanted to buy it, he was going to sell it to someone else. My Father Lyle and Uncle Amos, my dad's youngest brother was the only two that were interested. Uncle Amos was also getting an opportunity, at the same time to buy a grain company that he had worked for. He decided to put his money in the grain company. I would imagine that part of the reason he didn't buy it, was the 300 acres was not all cleared for farming and would require a lot of money to make it a grain farm. Daddy would have to go in debt not only for the farm, but for the clearing of it.

Grandpa was pleased that someone in the family wanted it as he had bought it from the state and no one else but our family had ever owned it. So, the island passed down another generation. There were still two other families living on the island at that time. Most of the others had moved across the levee in order to quit fighting the river every time it rose. The flood of 1937 had driven most of them away. There was one old man, who was like a hermit, that had put up a tent on a high spot which was actually on our farm boundary. Obviously, he had no idea he was on private property because he was in the tree line where we had finished clearing.

I would go down with Daddy to watch the progress and swing on the grapevines. Tarzan was a big star during this time frame all kids wanted to be Tarzan or Jane. When three of us played together, one had to be Cheetah, the monkey. Since I had mostly boy playmates no one wanted to be Jane, so I always had that position and never had to worry about being Cheetah. The boys would argue, and when it could not be decided who would be Tarzan, they would draw a line. Next, they would attempt to throw a rock past the line. The one who threw the farthest got the coveted position of Tarzan while the loser became Cheetah.

We had a little dog, named Pudgy who had some rat terrier blood that would run through the woods with me. I was old enough that no one was concerned about my safety. But then I had been a free spirit since I was 4 and managed to survive, so I guess they thought there was no reason to be concerned now.

On one of the trips, Pudgy and I were deep into the oaks and cypress that were always thick around the chute, when all of a sudden, I ran upon a King Snake! One of the largest I had ever seen, was coiled in the small path. This snake is a non- venomous snake and not very aggressive. It strangles its prey. It is called the king of snakes because they commonly feed on other snakes. This includes venomous snakes since they are immune to the venom. My Dad said he never liked to see people kill king snakes because they kept rats, mice and venomous snakes from being so plentiful. They are alarming to look at because of their size, but will not harm you unless you become aggressive!

I started to back out slowly keeping my eyes on the snake, as my dog was barking and jumping back and forth while getting closer and closer to the snake, which agitated it. He was such a fat little dog that he wasn't particularly fast. The snake coiled up and struck at the dog, which was quicker than I thought he could be and moved to the side. I was yelling 'Pudgy, come!" over and over. He kept up this irritating barking too long. The snake had gotten smarter, and the dog had gotten slower! This time the snake struck him! Although they are not venomous, they have sharp teeth. He bit the dog on the front right leg and recoiled immediately. The dog started yelping as he turned to run away with a terrible limp. I was far enough away to start running and the dog managed to follow me, yelping the whole way. When Daddy heard the dog, he drove across the field in his Willy's Jeep to where we were. He got some clean water and washed the dogs wound. The bite was shallow enough that when we got home, we put medication on it. He wrapped it and it healed without any problems.

I have always felt that the dog's attempt to combat the snake was to protect me. Once I was far enough away the dog was not as attentive to the snake, allowing him to get that chance to bite him. Many times, I have wished I had a camera to show how big this snake was. They grow up to 6 feet according to the statistics, and this one was much large than a six- foot snake which I had seen before. This one was very large around. It might have had an animal inside, that he was trying to digest, when we came upon him. He also had many coils. Additionally, there was the possibility that it was a female that was pregnant.

CHAPTER 19

DISCOVERING WHY PEOPLE WERE AFRAID OF MY FATHER

On our new farm there was a lot of tree-cutting and stump removal in order to be able to put in crops. One of the first things Daddy planted was corn. He was hopeful for a good crop this first year as it had cost a lot more to clear the farm than he had anticipated. He had hoped to sell a lot of the hardwood that was cut to help defray the cost. He was disappointed that he had more trees than the local timber buyers wanted, as several other farms were being cleared at the same time.

It was a beautiful early autumn afternoon when Daddy had asked me if I wanted to go look at the corn. I had nothing better to do, and this would mean a stop at the small grocery store where I could buy my favorite chocolate bar and get a Coke. Pudgy jumped in with us. He hung out of the window for 45 minutes it took us to drive there. After the grocery store treat, we went on to the island.

When we drove into the corn field, Daddy threw the brakes on. There were hogs everywhere eating the corn! He was furious! The Pointers, one of the few families left living on the island after the 1937 flood, had bought a lot of hogs. Daddy had asked if they would be penned up, and they had told him "Yes." They had not. There was no pen! They were letting their hogs eat our corn instead of feeding them.

Daddy drove up directly to the house where the two brothers lived. He jumped upon the porch and knocked on the door. Both brothers responded to the knock and appeared to be very nervous. He told them about the problem and reminded them that they had promised to pen them up. They said their truck had been broken down, so they could not pick up the fencing. One of them said now they had the truck repaired and he was going to town the next day to get it. They would get the fencing and put it up tomorrow. They said they were sorry about the corn loss. Daddy said the hogs looked "fat and sleek" thanks to all the corn they had ingested. He also said he did not want to see a single hog in his field when he came back. One of them said, "No sir, Mr. Lyle we'll take care of it."

Three days later, Daddy and I repeated the trip with the dog back to the corn field. This time the hogs were all over the field and some of the corn had been trampled down, or someone had cut it down so that the hogs would be able to get to the grain easier. Daddy jumped out of the Jeep before it even made a stop in front of their house! He ran up on the porch and started beating on the door!

Our dog was excited and jumped out. I got out to get the dog. Daddy turned and said "Get back in the Jeep and take the dog." I knew from his tone of voice that this was going to be bad. I picked up Pudgy which was no easy task as her name described the problem. She was so fat around it was hard to put my arms around her and pick her up. After struggling over to the Jeep, I managed to get her inside just in time to hear one of the brothers open the door and say "Why the hell are you beating on our door?" Daddy replied, "Because you're a lying Son-of-a-bitch. You had no intention of penning up those hogs. You're letting me fatten them up for you to make you money, while I'm losing money on my corn." Pen them up! I won't tell you again!" My daddy had never cursed in front of me. I knew that he had a bad reputation for violence. Other than mother and my shooting experience with him in December of 1954 I had never witnessed him when he was violent.

With that, the fellow slammed the door in Daddy's face and locked it. He closed the shutters in his house which made no way for Daddy to get to them. He turned around, looked at me, hesitated, then got in the Jeep. He said "I'm taking you home and I'll deal with this later." The ride home was quiet but fast. We were traveling way over the speed limit. It was so fast that the dog quit hanging out the window. He never said a word to me and his face was red with anger. He had a blood pressure problem which had kept him out of the second world war. I worried that he might have a stroke or heart attack. When he got home, he remained quiet the rest of the time, then went to bed early. He seemed somewhat more relaxed.

Now the Pointer brothers were trammel net fishermen. (A trammel net has 3 layers of net to catch fish. Fish can swim through the larger mesh but then get caught in the smaller inner mesh. They have a floating rope on top and a weighted rope on the bottom. When the fish try to escape, the two nets form a pocket that traps them. This was not "sport" fishing, this was for commercial purposes. Some states do not allow trammel nets as they take too many fish out at a time. This overfishing reduces some of the species so much that they become endangered.)

The Pointers checked the trammel net for the fish every morning then took their catch into a town across the river to sell. Before they left, they would reassemble the net for the next day. Daddy knew that they wouldn't be home until late in the day, so he got up early the next morning. I was reading a comic book while I was eating my breakfast and letting my egg get cold. It was Monday morning, a school day for me. Daddy was dressed and he walked out of his bedroom carrying a 22 Rifle that I often shot. I asked if he was going hunting. He said, "I guess you could call it that." I wondered if he was going back to see the Pointers and taking the gun for protection. It worried me because he had a terrible temper if you crossed him. The Pointers had done that. He got in the Jeep and left without saying good-bye to Mother or me. All day at school, I worried that they might have shot him or he might have shot them.

What I found out later is that he loaded the 22 Rifle, walked through the cornfields and shot every one of the hogs in the head. He left them where they fell, got back in his Jeep then came home. When I got home after school, Daddy and Mother had already come in from work at the farm equipment business. He was in a good humor. No mention was made of the Pointers. Mother was fixing supper while Daddy was reading the newspaper.

The front door bell rang. I opened the door to see the Pointer brothers on the other side of our locked screen door. The minute they saw me, one said, "Where's your old man?" I said," Daddy the Pointers are here to see you." He rose up slowly still holding his newspaper as he walked to the door. The minute they saw him, one of the called him a dirty name and was saying how he was going to "whip his ass", while the other one was yelling about how they were going to sue him, for killing their hogs. He turned to me and said calmly, "Go back to the kitchen with your mother." I walked down the hall by the bedrooms, but I didn't go to the kitchen. I ran into mother who was also standing in the hall listening. None of the three had a gun or knife. The Pointers had not attempted to open the screen door, so we didn't know what would happen next. There were two of them, but that had never been a problem in any encounter Daddy had in the past. He once had a man a lot larger than him attack him with a knife.

He had taken the knife away from him, and would have beaten him to death, except for the intervention of one of his brothers. I had heard that story around town many times. There were other stories that were very similar that had caused him encounters with the law. The word had always been, don't mess with Lyle. He is a dangerous man.

The Pointer older brother said, "You killed every one of our hogs with a bullet through the head." Daddy said, "You should thank me. I left the bodies intact where you could dress them out and put them up in your smokehouse for the winter. If you get back down there instead of standing on my porch, maybe the meat won't spoil".

There was silence. Then Daddy said, "I warned you both two times to pen those hogs up. The second time, I told you I would not tell you again. I'm a man of my word. I didn't tell you again, I took matters into my own hands and found my own solution."

One of the brothers said, "You're going to be sorry you ever met us. We're not going to let this just go away." Daddy said, "I'm already sorry that I met you. But if that is a threat, I want you to remember this. If you don't get off my porch, and go home to clean the hogs out of my field, the same thing will happen to you and unlike the hogs, I will not give you another warning."

With that Daddy threw open the screen door to step out. The two brothers backed up and one jumped off the porch, the other backed up too far and fell off the porch. The one on the ground, scrambled half crouched to the truck while the more agile one was already in the driver's seat starting the motor. As soon as the motor cranked, they put it in gear and left for the island.

Mother and I went to the kitchen. Daddy sat down and continued to read his paper. There was no mention of anything regarding the front door confrontation. When supper was ready, we all ate in silence. Mother didn't go to town that night. This was Daddy's last encounter with the Pointers as they moved off the island shortly after this happened. What the Pointers did with the hogs was a mystery. Their threat never came to fruition. Too many people who had lived on the island knew Daddy's reputation and although they were ignorant, they were not stupid.

CHAPTER 20

THE ASIAN FLU

In the summer of 1957, the Asian Flu came to the United States. It was a global pandemic which had originated in Guizhou in Southern China. There was a vaccine developed against it which they later found out was not as strong as it needed to be to produce immunity. I was 15 and one of those who received the vaccine, because of my medical background. Still, I ended up with the worst symptoms of the flu including pneumonia. For two weeks in 1958, I lay in bed sleeping about 20 hours a day. They would wake me up to feed me. I could not eat and keep the food down. I existed on liquids. My fever was always too high. The doctor kept telling them that I would begin to improve as I had received the vaccine. After the two weeks, it was as though I was in a coma. I could not walk when they got me up.

My Dad said he was taking me to the hospital and not calling the doctor again. He picked me up and carried me to the car. When we arrived at the hospital, they discovered I had pneumonia and had lost 15 pounds. I was hospitalized for another two weeks before they could get me strong enough to sit up. Having had tuberculosis at the age of 5, they were fearful of a reoccurrence, so they limited my physical activity for another month at home, until I got stronger. This episode hurt my immunity more than we knew at the time.

The flu did give me the opportunity to do something I needed to learn. When I was hanging around the house, resting and minding the doctor's orders and bored, Daddy came in the house. He said "I'm going to take you out and teach you to drive." He had a grey Willy's Jeep that he had bought second hand from an Army Surplus. It had a four- speed transmission which requires a clutch to use when you change the gears. You started the Jeep with your left foot on the clutch while you pulled the gear shift which was in the floor board down to the left. Then let your foot off the clutch slowly as you pressed your foot on the accelerator. Then you pushed the clutch down again as you increased your speed and changed it to the second gear up to the right. Next you pushed the clutch down and pulled the gear shift straight down to the 4th gear which was the fastest position. To back up, you engaged the clutch and pushed it up to the left. If you let your foot off the clutch too quickly on any of these gear changes, the motor would stall, and you would have to start all over. If you didn't hold the clutch down all the way and moved the gear shift, a loud grinding noise would occur. (Mother always had a new car and in my whole life, I have driven her car twice. She allowed me to drive it to practice parallel parking. Then I used it to take my driver's test. I guess she thought the Jeep would not pass an inspection.)

Daddy and I drove into the 120 acres field behind our house, where the two big barns were. He showed me how to use the gear shift and the clutch to change gears. Then I was put behind the wheel. After four attempts, I finally managed to make the Jeep move forward, so that I might try to get it to the second gear, without making the motor stall. We were driving in the field and over the rows where the crops had been taken out. We bounced across the field as there were no smooth spots except the dirt road through the middle of the farm. We practiced for over an hour when Daddy told me to go back toward the house. When we got to the house, he got out and said, "Take the Jeep and drive it until all your gear changes are smooth and it doesn't stall or grind when you shift the gears anymore. Don't come back to the house until you have perfected it. Then you can take me for a ride." I said, "What if I hit one of the barns?" He said, "Lydia, if you can't miss two barns, in a 120 acres field, you will never be able to get your license." Then he laughed and walked off. I bounced over those crop rows until it was almost dark. My bottom was sore as Jeep's manufacturer was not interested in the comfort of the driver. When I finally honked the horn to pick him up, I could drive!

CHAPTER 21

BOYFRIENDS ENTER MY LIFE

I had my first date with a boy two years older than me in the autumn of 1958 when I was 15 years old. He was on the football team and had beautiful red hair and brown eyes. I was excited about going! I wanted to look my best, as I had a big crush on him so I wanted everything to be perfect. He had invited me to go to the movie in another town. He picked me up in a pick-up truck that belonged to his grandfather. It had the name of the grocery store that his family owned on the side doors. When you went to the movie, you dressed up. I had worn a white blouse with a navy- blue skirt. I had worked with my hair and my make-up so I would look perfect. We were driving along visiting and getting acquainted through a rural area. It was a hot day and we had the windows rolled down as the truck had no air conditioning. The music was playing on the radio, so all was good.

As we were going around a large curve a bird was chasing another in front of us. They were not paying attention to the on-coming truck and suddenly changed direction toward us. The first bird which was smaller and was being chased, quickly moved upward and over the top of the truck. The second bird which was a hawk but much larger didn't fly up fast enough and hit the rearview mirror on my side of the truck. Blood and feathers flew everywhere! The majority came in the window on me. Blood splattered in my face and hair and all over what had been my white blouse. I did not know whether to laugh or cry. My date was more upset than I was when he saw all the blood. He was afraid I was hurt. We turned around and he took me home, to a lot of explaining to my parents about what had happened. This is not the kind of first date that you reminisce about. I did date him after that and later attended my first prom with him. I dated several other boys through high school but nothing is ever as memorable as your first boyfriend.

I had gone to my first school party in the eighth grade. I was taller than most of the boys in my class. I had hoped that one of the tall boys would ask me to the dance. I had a crush on one of these tall boys that started in the first- grade. I got into a fuss with another girl about him in class. The teacher had made me and the other girl go sit in the hall. We were to wait for Miss Tanner, the principal that I had developed a fear of when I had thrown the little girl off the merry-go-round, the first day of school.

Miss Tanner had a large paddle she carried around and she had already told me that she didn't want to see me in trouble, again. This time I was afraid I was going to find out how badly the paddle hurt. She asked us why we were sitting outside the class room door. The other girl said nothing so I said very quickly "I was talking to Robbie and asked him to be my boyfriend" and she said, "No, he's my boyfriend" and I said, "He didn't say so," and there was the teacher standing over us telling us to go to the hall and sit down. Miss Tanner said "Lydia, why do you think she said that?" I said "Because we weren't supposed to talk in class?" Then she said to the other girl, "What do you think the reason was?" She said, "I don't know because he is my boyfriend." To which I said, "He didn't say so." That was when I learned not to keep talking. She told me to stand up and she hit me lightly with the paddle and it stung. She made the other girl stand up and did the same thing to her. She told us both to go back into the class-room and if we opened our mouths again, we would get three hard licks each. Neither one of us cried, but I shut up for the rest of the year and decided she could have Robbie. This first- grade crush turned out to be one of the two tall boys in my class that I hoped would take me to the dance.

After suffering pain from Miss Tanner's paddle and being humiliated, because of him in first grade, I was dejected about his not asking me to the 8th grade party. However, he did not go with the other girl who claimed him as her boyfriend either. A boy who was a lot shorter than me asked me to go. My mother and Daddy said I had to go since he asked me. It was a casual affair and I wore a lime full skirt with crinolines under it with a lime and white striped blouse to match. My mother picked him up, and it was a typical school party for young people. Girls on one side, boys on the other. On the way home, in the back seat of my mother's car, he surprised me by leaning over and kissing me on the mouth. That was my first kiss and once again, it was not something you reminisce about. Mother saw him do that in the rear- view mirror and I was embarrassed. All I could think about was, "I didn't even like him, and had been forced to go with him to the party. Now he would be telling others he had kissed me!"

CHAPTER 22

THE DEBATE DEBACLE

In high school, I participated in clubs, plays, band, was a good student, member of the honor society and a member of a debate team throughout my high school years.

The debate team was one of my favorites. The team had arranged to debate a group of other schools from a larger town with an award being presented at the conclusion. It was an all-day affair and we were to dress up in our best, the guys in sportscoats with ties, and the girls in dresses, heels, and hose.

The morning of the debate, I looked in my closet and I could not find anything other than skirts, blouses and sweaters. I was subscribed to a magazine that showed teenagers in the city wearing the latest fashions. I also looked at Aunt Ann's "Vogue" magazine of grown women's clothes in New York. My dresses were church dresses and had no sophistcation that I thought a debater should have. Mother had already gone to work, so I walked into her room and looked in her closet. I was taller than her and weighed a little more, but I thought I might find something she had worn to conventions or special outings. Hanging there in a plastic bag was a taupe straight knit dress with a matching jacket. I don't think it had been worn yet so she must have bought it for a special occasion. It looked "classy," so I thought even if I didn't win the debate, I would be the best dressed. Then, shoes were the next problem as I only had two pairs of heels. Neither was appropriate for this stunning look. Mother and I wore the same size shoes.

Mother had a fetish for expensive shoes and coats. I remembered that she had a pair of real lizard heels with a matching purse. I put on her real pearls that Daddy had given her for her birthday a few years before. I knew If I called to ask her to wear these clothes the answer would be "No." I also knew that I would be home before she came from work. I would have my boyfriend drop me at the house, and I would put all this up before she returned.

I slipped on the dress and it fitted perfectly. I put on my makeup before I fixed my hair. I added the pearls and earrings. I looked at myself in the mirror, and I looked like "college" instead of high school. A friend of mine picked me up to take me to school. She said, "Wow, where'd you get that dress?" I told her out of the closet. I didn't bother to tell her it wasn't my closet.

We left early on the school bus and arrived at 9 o'clock for a breakfast reception as well as an opportunity to meet the other teams we were to debate. This was to be over at 10am as our team was to be in the first debate.

One team was missing. We waited until 10 and did not hear from them. The town they were coming from was 32 miles away. One of the teachers called their school, and they were told that the bus had left on time and should have arrived at about 9:30, at the latest. This was the team that we were to debate. Another 30 minutes came and passed with no team. 11:00 came and the teacher called the school again. They told us that they had sent someone to drive down the highway to check out what could have happened. They also were going to call the state patrol as a precaution. A little before 11:30 we heard from the state patrol. They explained that they had found the bus, and the decision had been made to take the bus back to their hometown school. Later, someone came out to tell us that we would not be debating that day as we would have no one to debate.

The patrolman told us that as the team was riding south to meet us, one of the boys riding on the bus took out a sign from his book bag. He unfolded it and placed it in the back window of the bus. He said, "I want to see if this will work" and he laughed. No one had seen what was written on the paper. The sign said, "Bus Driver Gone Berserk, Call the State Patrol." Apparently, the first few people who saw the sign didn't take it seriously. Not easily deterred, he started waving his arms frantically when a car would come close or pass. Finally, someone believed it and turned off at the first place they could find a phone to call the authorities.

When the bus came down out of the hilly part of the area, several state patrol and police from surrounding towns had put up a road block, and traffic was backed up on the two- lane highway. With guns drawn they entered the bus while telling everyone to get off. They stood the bus driver up to put handcuffs on him. They questioned him about whether he had threatened any of the students on the bus. When they were convinced that he was not "berserk" they turned to look at the students. When they were confident that the bus was emptied out, they asked who had put up the sign. Everyone acted like no one knew what they were talking about. The boy had hidden the sign in the bus before the patrol came on board. They searched until they found it stuffed beneath a seat. Once it was found, they began to interrogate all the students who had been onboard. After a long period of denying it, the patrol told them what serious punishment there would be for bringing out the state patrol, plus all of the police and other authorities for a false threat.

Finally, someone confessed who had done it. The students were from a college town and the culprit was the son of the college president. It was too late by the time they had finished with questioning the students for them to continue with our debate. They had taken the culprit to the Sheriff's Office in his home town for him to wait, until his parents arrived, to confront them with the problem and the resulting fine.

Our opponents had to forfeit their debate. All the other schools went ahead as usual which meant we were not going to arrive home on time. As I sat there while the other towns did their debates, I began to squirm in my seat. This meant that Mother was going to be home by the time I arrived home and I was going to be in trouble. I had left the plastic bag her dress had come in on her bed, and if she had any doubts about what had happened to it, she would know when I walked in the door. Also, I had left the box the shoes had come in on the floor. The shoes were my biggest concern. Mother cherished this particular pair of shoes and matching purse. I hoped I had not done any damage to them.

When I finally got to the house and walked in, she was sitting in the kitchen waiting. (I felt as though I was a fly walking into a spider web! I had been caught and she was a big old black widow spider waiting to wrap me up.) She was livid! She said "What were you thinking? That whole outfit is brand new, and I was saving it for something special! There is nothing special about today that you needed to wear something this expensive to high school." I said, "I'm sorry but my dresses all look like church clothes." Mother said, "That's because they are, and you don't need anything out of my closet for any of the places you are going. Don't ever take anything out of my closet to wear again. Take my dress off and my shoes and keep in mind, they are not yours! If anything is damaged, you will be grounded!" I took the dress off and attempted to hang it back up and sat down on the bed to remove the shoes. The purse and shoes appeared to be undamaged. I never tried that again.

My best friend, Edith had pretty clothes, and we wore the same size, so she and I started swapping our clothes, which I'm sure made my mother happy, and satisfied the two of us.

CHAPTER 23

THE WILD SIDE

During the late 1950's and early 1960's, teenagers did things that now would be considered vandalism. But at that time, it was considered a "prank." The difference between the two is that a "prank" instead of becoming a police problem, became a parental problem. If you were picked up for underage drinking most likely the police would take you to the station and call your parents. They would pay a fine then take you home where you would be punished.

There was only 27 miles between my hometown and a wild town across the river. That town had a lot of corruption including mafia that came from Chicago, Illinois to hide out there. There were all kinds of night clubs, illegal gambling, prostitution, and liquor sold to minors in that city. When I was 15, I had gone with an older male cousin who was 21, his girlfriend, and a male friend of mine who was 16, to see a rock and roll performer named Ray Smith at one of these clubs. Smith had a hit called "Rocking Little Angel" which climbed the charts to #22 and was the only hit of his lifetime. My parents thought I was going to the movie with this group.

I was really nervous as they checked us through the front

door. The place was packed with other underage kids. I looked around and couldn't see anyone I knew, because of the heavy smoke that was dimming the lighting on the inside of the building. Smith's crew was putting the instruments and other items on the stage. My nervousness turned to excitement when I realized I was here to see a "Star." Once seated, a waitress came up to ask what kind of a drink, we all would like to have. I had no clue. I had spent 11 years of my life with an alcoholic who only drank bourbon straight.

Everyone was ordering something off the bulletin board in front of the bar. I looked at the list when the waitress said, "What would you like?" I really would have liked to have a Coke but it wasn't on the board. I didn't want to hesitate as I feared they would ask me for an ID. I looked up above the bar and saw a drink with a little umbrella in it and thought, "That can't be very strong, it looks like a kids drink." I said "I'll have a Singapore Sling." Big mistake! One drink and I knew it was stronger than I could stand. I didn't have to worry too long about drinking it because someone yelled, "The police are outside and they're going to raid the place!" Someone had told the police that all these underage teenagers would be at this club tonight because of Smith's performance. The performance was about to start so they knew the place was packed, so this would be the time for the raid. We were sitting next to the rest rooms, far away from the door which the police were just entering. My cousin's date said, come on we've got to get out of here. Upon entering the bathroom, we saw a small window and opened it up so that we could slip outside. We heard a man's voice say, "If there are any girls in the stalls, we want them to come out now." We were laying back flat against the building and had shut the window behind us. He looked out into the darkness but did not open the window. The moment he left the bath room, we began running toward the wooded field behind us. We stayed in the woods until all the police had left. The girl said, "I'm afraid we might step on a snake in these woods." I was more afraid of my parents than I was of any snake, so I stayed put and she did, too. After all the cars had left, except those people who were of legal age, we saw my cousin driving by looking for us. We could hear "Rocking Little Angel" coming out of the club. I don't remember what happened to my date, but he was in the car when my cousin picked us up. I never attempted this again, although a lot of kids from my town, and other surrounding towns went there regularly. My parents never found out, and I never tried to go again.

CHAPTER 24

HALLOWEEN AND PRANKS

Pranks were a different problem. Halloween in particular. When you live in a rural area, there are plenty of people who still have an outhouse. On Halloween, some of the boys would take the outhouse off its foundation, use their pick- up to put it on a trailer or drag it to someone's yard they didn't like. Sometimes they set it up in the middle of the street downtown. It was a busy night for the police as we only had one patrol car, and it was difficult for them to be everywhere they needed to be. The teenagers took advantage of this, just this one night a year.

My dad had gotten rid of his gray Willy's Jeep and purchased a two- tone green Jeep truck instead. It was an ugly truck, both in construction and color. The interior was very uncomfortable but it was "wheels and freedom." When I got my license, he let me drive at night anytime I wanted. Mother did not want me out running up and down the streets nor going to other towns in the Jeep. She had told me I couldn't drive it except when she said so. I believe she was afraid she would run into me with her boyfriend like she had done several years before. Also, she refused to ever let me drive her car so I was pretty blue about the whole matter of having a license and no ability to use it. One night Daddy said,

"On the nights your mother leaves to visit her girlfriends, you can use the truck to go to town after you finish your homework and your piano practice. We'll wait until your mother leaves, then you must be back here before she returns." I did this every time she left, and she never caught me until Halloween in 1960.

Halloween was the wildest night of the year! I left the house in the Jeep as soon as mother left the garage. I was in a hurry to pick up my friend Edith and her younger sister, Ellie. Another friend of Ellie's wanted to go with us so we would pick her up later. When I pulled up to their house, Edith hopped in and I thought Ellie was all the way in the truck and started off. Ellie started yelling! I threw the brake on. She had one foot in the truck and one on the ground, that she was attempting to run on while hanging on the door with her hands. We pulled her to safety and picked up her good friend, Callie. We all thought it was funny, which shows you how immature we are when we are teenagers.

Callie was a pretty little blond from a large family who was high spirited enough to run with us. She and Ellie got in the bed of the truck, and we started riding around town. We were checking on what was going to be the "talk of the town" tomorrow. Some of the boys had already bought a lot of eggs and were driving by each other, while throwing the eggs at their opponent. Somebody else had already set up an outhouse on one street, and some other boys had dropped bails of straw on several streets before setting fire to them. One of them dared me to drive over the flaming bale (never could resist a dare), and I did, but the undercarriage of the Jeep dragged the bale that was on fire down the road with me. I was in a state of panic and made several wild turns finally managing to dislodge it! I decided that wasn't one of my better ideas, so I didn't repeat it. We took off for the grocery store to buy some eggs. There were three grocery stores and the first store had only one carton of eggs left.

About that time another girl from our class drove by in her mother's car with her windows down. She was always dressed "prim and proper" and would never have "run" with us. That was an invitation to egg her and she knew it. She soon turned around to go back home. We decided to egg her later when she came back through town. A few minutes later here came her car. I turned the Jeep around so that we could get a clean shot as I passed her. As I pulled up even with her, the girls in the back were going to throw the eggs, when I realized it was not her. Instead, it was her mother, who had no sense of humor. Edith turned quickly, beating on the window and shaking her head frantically, "No," so they wouldn't throw them. They saw Edith and laid down in the truck bed. I slowed down and eased behind her, following her car until the next turn. We only had a dozen eggs and three of them were broken when the girls laid down on top of them.

Disappointed by this failed encounter, we had decided to try and buy some more eggs. The boys had tried twice to intercept us with their eggs, to no avail. But we were running out of time to get any ammunition to fight them. We stopped at the other two grocers that were open at night and neither had any left. I said, "I have an idea. (Again, this was not one of my better ideas.) Let's get a bucket of lard and some flour. We'll make a ball of the lard and roll it in the flour. We'll throw them at the windshield and windows of the pick-ups and when they land, they'll splatter flour and grease on the glass, so they won't be able to see us to throw the eggs." I didn't think about the fact that the "lard balls" would not be heavy enough to throw very far. When the boys came around the corner, they started hitting us with their eggs, we retaliated with the few eggs we had left, and the "lard balls." We managed to hit the windshield, but not the side glass, so I sped off and headed for home to hide in the garage so we might regroup with a better idea. The boys were in "hot pursuit." We had a two- car garage with manual overhead doors and knew we had to reach the garage in order to pull the doors down to keep them out.

Both sides of the door were up. I drove quickly into the left side, and all four of us jumped out to pull down the doors. Edith and I got the left door down, but Ellie and Callie were not quick enough, and the boys pulled into the right side of the garage where they unloaded their whole supply of eggs on us and the Jeep! I was wishing I had not left the garage light on. They would have had difficulty seeing us in the dark, and we could have hidden under the Jeep. Too late! We were throwing the "lard balls" back at them, but we were getting drenched by the eggs, while trying to get close enough to do them any damage. We had eggs on our clothes and eggs in our hair running down our faces and dripping to the floor. The inside walls of the garage were splattered with eggs and shells that had stayed stuck. We managed to get a little of the lard and flour on the boys as they approached us, but we ran out of ammunition before they did. This started a lot of laughing and carrying on, until my dad stuck his head inside the side door to the porch.

The boys all knew his reputation and immediately stopped what they were doing to head for their truck. He told them not to get in the truck. He said, "All of you are going to help clean up this mess before Ava gets home." He apparently struck fear in them, because all four of them said "Yes Sir." He handed two of them a broom and the other two some water hoses to hook up. No one said a word or tried to leave. He told me to get some rags, a bucket and detergent out of the house and for the girls to start cleaning the outside of the Jeep. He said, "If you don't get all of the eggs off it will ruin the paint. My thought was "Good, I hate that color paint, but I did not say it." We began the clean-up. The girls and the boys got the job done, but not before Mother arrived. The floor was still slick from all the eggs and especially the lard that hadn't reached the truck. She stepped out of her car and surveyed the "war zone." Mother then made us reclean everything. Afterwards, I took my friends home and came home to a grounding that lasted for a month. Mother asked why I was driving the Jeep when I was not supposed to go out without her permission. Daddy said "It is Halloween and they were just trying to have a good time. I let her go out to celebrate with her friends, so she had my permission. It did get out of control but it's all cleaned up now and no harm was done. (Or so he thought.)" Mother was mad, but she didn't give up without grounding me for a month.

Next morning at school, we were all talking about what had transpired the night before. Mid-morning the principal came into the classroom, and asked Edith and me to come to the Assembly Hall. When we walked in, we were standing on the stage when the principal told us the police were coming to see us. I looked at Edith, and I thought she was going to cry. I said "Don't cry, whatever it is they will think we're guilty." I was waiting to see if there was anything to cry about. Edith said, "My Dad's going to be so mad!" She was my best friend and would follow me on my crazy adventures anywhere, anytime. My Dad wouldn't be too upset, but my mother would probably ground me for the rest of the year. Neither of us knew what the problem was, but we were soon to find out.

We owned the only green two- toned Jeep in town. Someone in a green Jeep had taken a chain and wrapped around several concrete markers which were used to mark our streets. The markers looked like an obelisk and were very attractive. Some of them had been dropped at the place they were unearthed but some of them had disappeared. The policeman said, "Lydia, you're in trouble for stealing and damaging city property. Edith, you're an accomplice." I said what have we done wrong. He explained about the obelisks. I said, "We didn't do that." Edith said, "No Sir, we didn't."

He said he had been told by a citizen they had seen a green Jeep pulling the markers up, and we had the only Green Jeep in town. I also said, "I don't believe Edith and I could wrap a chain around them and pull them up, as I don't have a chain. We're certainly not strong enough to load and carry them off." I told him about the eggs, the people we were with, and where we were at that time. He said he wondered about how four girls would do this without help. He walked out of the hall, and we were sent back to class. Our prissy friend was smirking when we walked in, and I was sorry we hadn't hit her with the eggs. I dreaded going home, because I knew the police were headed to our house, when they left to verify what we had told them. I don't remember if they went to Edith's house, too.

When I got home Daddy said, "Lydia, the police have been here and I know you did not do what the police accused you of, but you are never going out for another Halloween ride. They also told me that you were dragging a bale of straw that was afire through town." I told him about the fire, and he told me that it was extremely dangerous to do what I had done. He also said, "I thought you had more sense than that." He also told me my driving privileges would be over, if I did any other crazy things.

Upon checking, the police found a young man from a surrounding town with his two buddies were guilty of the crime. He had a solid green Jeep truck, and they were caught with the obelisks, still in the truck bed. The police came to our house and told my dad that they were mistaken. However, that didn't shorten my grounded time.

CHAPTER 25

MY SENIOR YEAR

All of a sudden, all the high school pranks and vandalism had come to a halt. I had no clue where I was going with my life. I decided to cram in everything I could into this one last year. The school had a theater production so I tried out and got a part in a play that was a murder mystery. This meant having to rehearse nightly, then go home to do my homework, before I went to bed. This was such a shock to my sleep routine that had been established at the age of 6. Because of the need for me to get plenty of rest so that I might not get Tuberculosis again, my bedtime was always 9 pm during the week for the school months and 11 pm on the week- ends. When someone would invite me for a sleepover, they would have to keep me up as I would drift off to sleep about 9:30 pm.

The irregular routine of the play caused me to have insomnia because after 12 at night I would be wide awake until 3 am or 4 am in the morning. Then I would have to get up at 6 am to get ready for school. After the play was over, I thought I would be able to go back to sleep on my regular schedule at 9, but it didn't happen.

The year went quickly by, and the spring came. A boyfriend

named Bob that I had dated in the past, had gone off to college to study engineering. He called and asked me to come to the St. Pat's Party in March. His fraternity's dorm was going to be made into the "hotel" for the girls from out of town. There was a lady that would be our chaperone for the weekend. We would spend two nights there while the boys bunked elsewhere. I was excited about going and needed a dress to wear that fitted the occasion.

A lady in town, named Miss Hooper had sewn for me, since I was a small child, and was still making me formals for school proms and parties. I wanted to buy a pattern that looked sophisticated and sexy. I had never owned anything like that. Miss Hooper had never made something like that for anyone, as far as I knew. The pattern I picked had a scoop neckline which barely showed the top of your breasts. The material for the top was a patterned green on green taffeta. The skirt was a full cocktail length chiffon in the lighter green of the top pattern. Miss Hooper took one look at the pattern and said, "This top looks awfully low for a young lady." I said, "I want to wear it to a college party, so I don't want to look like a little girl." When we went for my fitting on the dress, it was exactly what I wanted. The only problem was Miss Hooper kept trying to pull the front up over my breasts.

I was to leave for the party with some other girls and was fully packed except for my party dress. I ran by Miss Hooper's to pick it up and went home, laid it on my bed so that I might get my matching shoes to see if it all matched. The shoes were perfect, but when I went to put the dress in the carrying bag, there was a "dickey" sewn across the top where the scoop neck was. It was the material left from the liner for the chiffon skirt. I was furious! I stripped off my clothes and threw the dress on and looked in the mirror and screamed! This brought both my parents to my room. I said, "Look what she's done to my dress." My Dad said "What? I think it looks pretty." I knew, from that moment on, I would never trust a man to tell me how I looked in any outfit. I turned to my mother and said, "I am not going to go to a college party with a dickey covering up my breasts, how embarrassing." Surprisingly, she said, "I'll get my sewing kit and take it out." She did.

The party was all "greened up" for St. Pat's with the food, beer and beverages all tinted green. I met a lot of Bob's friends as well as their girlfriends, and we had a "big time".

Totally exhausted, but excited about what I had just experienced, I was unaware of what I was about to discover when we returned to our rooms. I was taking my jewelry off and laid it down next to a letter that Bob was composing for his mother. There was no attempt to keep the letter private, so I think he wanted to make sure I saw it. In it he told his mother that he was in love with me and wanted to get engaged. He said he was going to Lavalier me the day after the dance when other members of the fraternity would be placing a Lavalier on their girlfriends. This would indicate they were seriously interested in going steady or getting engaged. I was not only upset, I felt like I had a big ball of wax in my stomach. I had come to party and have a good time. I had no plans to marry or get engaged at the age of 17. I didn't even want to go steady. What was I going to do?

I started reminiscing about my experiences with Bob, and what I might have done that led him to believe I wanted to marry him. Several things flashed through my mind, but none so vividly as the week-ends at the river with his family. I thought back about the previous years, when he was still in high school. Bob and I had dated for a period of time, going to movies and parties with friends. We also attended church with his family near the farm where they lived. I began to wonder if his asking me to the family campout might have been a clue that he wanted to be more than just a friend and a date. He was going on a fly- fishing trip with his parents and 2 younger brothers, who were all in attendance, when I was asked along. His mother was lovely to me and I thought she probably appreciated having another female for company. Bob loved teaching me to fly-fish, and I did enjoy it. My only prior fishing had been done with a cane pole on the banks of the island, sitting in the shade on a five- gallon bucket, or jug fishing with my dad which was not a sport.

Bob and I would spend the whole day casting or tying "flies" for the hooks that were used for bait. When the evening came, everyone would come back to the campsite before dusk then clean all the fish that had been caught that day. The entrails and scrap pieces were cast into the water where the boats were kept. The fish scraps would be eaten by other fish or animals during the night. Bob's mother would have a fabulous meal for all of us each night and after all of us cleaned up the dishes, we would play games until bedtime. We would get up the next day to repeat the same thing again.

One evening after dinner, we had a storm coming up. Everyone went down to the boats to help pull them on shore to tie them up. Everyone was working using flashlights to see. When the largest boat was pulled from the water, there were so many snakes eating the fish remains underneath it that you couldn't count them! When the light hit them, they thrashed around on top of each other seemingly undecided about which way to go. It was frightening to be in the dark looking at so many snakes in one spot. I had been taught not to be afraid of snakes, but this was very scary due to the darkness and the surprise they caused when the boat was moved! All of a sudden, they disappeared down into the water!

The boats were secured and we went into the cabins just in time to miss the heavy wind and rain. We all said good night and went to bed, exhausted by the full day in the outdoors plus knowing we had to be up to do it again the next day. I still had the insomnia problem and was very restless. I didn't sleep well because the snakes reminded me of recurring dreams that had suddenly ceased when I was 16. Now I was afraid this might make them return.

Coming back to reality after running through these memories, I made my decision. I truly enjoyed Bob's company and his family but I did not want to marry him. I felt no deep love for him and my future was in front of me. I did not want to embarrass him in front of the fraternity by refusing to accept the lavalier, so I decided to talk to him about it before the next day. This would be before the lavalier was going to be hung around my neck. When I approached him about it, I told him that I had read the letter to his mother. I asked him if he had left it out for me to see, because he was afraid to ask me if I was in love with him. He said, "Yes." I told him I liked him and enjoyed his company a lot but was not in love with him. He told me he was in love with me then asked me if I would accept the lavalier just as a present for our friendship. He said he was sorry he had not told me, but I might change my mind and decide to marry him, later. He said he would be too embarrassed to tell his fraternity brothers that he would not be placing his Lavalier. He looked as though he was going to cry and I did not want to hurt him further, so I said I would accept it as a friendship token. He hugged me making me wonder what I had done. I didn't want other boys back at school to not ask me for a date, because they thought I had a serious relationship with Bob. I wanted to go to the Prom and the school parties my senior year, and this could be an impediment. I didn't sleep all night, tossing and turning with guilt, about whether or not I had led him on to believe there was a future for us.

The Greek ceremony the next day was very short, and his fraternity's Greek letters were on a beautiful chain. Each man said something personal to the girl he had chosen. Bob placed the necklace around my neck and said something to me that I do not remember. Then he kissed me on the lips. My mind was racing so fast that I did not hear him, because I was worried about how you get "un-lavaliered" if there is such a word.

I had come to the party with girl-friends, but it had been

arranged for me to return home with Bob. On the way home that day, neither one of us said much. I was wearing the lavalier so I decided to tell him my plans for my future. I told him that I planned to apply at a private girl's college which was about 95 miles from his school. During the upcoming months I planned to go to school functions and parties with a date from my hometown. I knew he could not attend these functions due to school rules and the distance he would have to travel to do so. He listened in silence and finally said he was sorry he had put this pressure on me. I felt so bad for him but felt it would be unfair to continue with this charade.

I offered to give the lavalier back and he said he didn't want it, just do with it as I pleased. I took it off and put it into the box it had been stored in. I laid it on the seat between us. Bob looked at it, then picked it up and threw it out the window. I was shocked! The rest of the ride home seemed like an eternity. There was no conversation between us and when we reached my house, he got out of the car, unloaded my things and carried them to the back door. He turned around without a word said, went back to the car and left. As I watched him drive away, I hoped I had not made a mistake. I also hoped he would find the right woman for him.

I dated several boys in high school. One was the captain of the basketball team and a true gentleman. He was a tall brunette named David, with a sweet disposition who was a pleasure to be with. Another one was in my class named Jack who was a real romantic and wanted me to date only him. I was still dating both of these boys when one night I had a date with David. We had pulled into the driveway of my home and parked the car by the garage. We were just visiting and waiting for my dad to flash the garage lights off and on to indicate I should come in. All of a sudden, a large car zoomed up beside us. Jack jumped out and ran to the driver's side of David's car. He yelled for me to get out and told David to leave! With that, he started to yank open the car door on David's side. David said, "No" and locked the car doors.

I suppose Jack was full of testosterone, as he took his fist and hit David's windshield, which broke the window. With that, David's sweet disposition disappeared! This was his father's car and he knew he was in trouble. He jumped out of the car and started fighting with Jack! I could see this was going to be a one-sided fight, as David was 6'3" tall, very athletic and about 200 lbs. Jack was about 5'9" tall and about 140 lbs. All this noise got my father's attention and he came out to separate the boys. He told me to get out of the car and go in the house.

As I walked away, I was so shocked that I was almost in a daze. This was a side of Jack and David that I had never seen. It was good that Daddy had come out when he heard the ruckus. David was so much bigger than Jack, he would probably have hurt him badly. My Dad told them both to go home or he would call their parents. He told Jack he owed David's dad a new windshield. The boys anger began to cool down. I was watching all this drama through the venetian blinds as they both drove off and wondered what would happen next.

When Daddy came in, he was cross. He told me to go sit down, then asked me what caused the fight. I told him that Jack wanted me to just date him and was mad because I was with David. I also had told them both, I did not want to go steady and this seemed to be alright with David, but I did not realize that Jack was upset about it. During the 50's and 60's "going steady" seemed to be the thing every couple wanted to do. Daddy said, "You need to decide which one to date, as I understand what the problem is with these two young men. Have your decision made by tomorrow." I thought about it all night, and I ended up choosing Jack.

CHAPTER 26

COLLEGE BOUND

In November, 1960, my dad gave me a 1961 white Mercury Monterrey convertible for the good grades I had all through school. It had a gold and white leather interior and a white top. If you had ordered a special car made from Ford at the time, you could get a medallion that had your name on it. Mine said "Made especially for Lydia Constantine by Ford Motor Company," on the glove box. I was elated! When I went to pick up my friends for a ride, no one believed it was mine. If I hadn't had my name on the glove box, I would have not been able to convince some of my friends. The two- tone green ugly Jeep truck had been my mode of transportation all the way through high school. I put 40,000 miles on it and everyone associated me with the Jeep. The convertible was out of character but I managed to adjust to the change. It was hard to tell if mother was happy about it, but Daddy had made a promise and he never reneged. It was cold the day I got the convertible. I drove straight to Edith's house and picked her up. We rode around in our coats, hats and gloves with the top down. What a happy day!

All of a sudden, it was early May and school graduation was coming up. I had received my acceptance from the private girl's college. I don't know if I had "Senioritis" but I seemed to be developing a haughty attitude about everything. I had developed a snobby disposition and had there been more time at home I probably would have been unbearable. Maybe it was the convertible, no other girl in town had one. Very few kids had cars in the 1960s. Senior graduation gifts were beginning to arrive and I, along with 9 others of my classmates had received a scholarship to another college in the state. I would not be using mine because of the enrollment in the private college. An official from the college had come down for my interview. He told me about a young lady in a town nearby that I should contact about being a possible roommate. I had that on my list of things to do as soon as school dismissed. I also had a physical that was required for my college that had to be completed right away. It was scheduled for the Monday after graduation. I was so busy receiving gifts and writing thank you cards for wonderful things like, 2 pairs of silk pajamas, one with a monogram, expensive blouses, a gorgeous robe and jewelry. All this luxury of the car, private college and expensive gifts enhanced my stuck- up disposition that I was developing. I was soon to be humbled.

Graduation came and went, followed by parties all around town. Monday came and Mother took me to a nearby town where the physical was to be administered. The doctor came in and said things looked fine, but I seemed to be a little anemic and thin. Next, I had a chest ex-ray then after a while, an older doctor came in to look at the x-rays and listen to my chest. He turned to mother and said, "We'll contact you tomorrow with the results."

CHAPTER 27

MOTHER'S BETRAYAL

We went home and Mother seemed to be herself while riding in the car. When I got home, I went in my car to pick up my best friend, Edith. She received the same scholarship I had and was going to attend that college. It happened to be in the same town as the private one I was attending. Our plan was when I completed the two- year private school, I would join her at the university to finish. We were having a leisurely summer evening talking about our plans, riding around town with the top down. All the kids congregated at a local soda shop that we had frequented for years. We joined them and listened to everyone's plans for the future.

The next day, Tuesday, I slept late and when lunch time came, Mother and Daddy came home and said they had heard from the doctor and my tests were fine. They both acted so glum, but I thought perhaps they were not getting along. This worried me because Mother had always said she was going to get a divorce once I went off to college. Nothing had been said about that in years, so I dismissed the idea.

Mother liked to go to town and visit with a lot of different businesses during the day when they were not both busy at the office. She had spent Wednesday and Thursday doing that. I went to the usual hang outs and a couple of times, I felt as though people were talking about me. I had no idea why. Thursday night, Mother said I needed to pack my clothes because I had to go to the Tuberculosis Sanatorium that Daddy had been to and have some additional tests run. I said, "When did you find this out?" She said the older doctor that I had been to on Monday had come to practice pulmonary medicine in our area. He was foreign and had been practicing at the Sanatorium for a few years. Our doctor had called him in because he saw a spot on my x-ray below the clavicle on my left lung, which looked suspicious. When he called the next day, he said we needed to have some tests done, then Mother had suggested the Sanatorium because Daddy had such good results there. These tests would leave no question of whether or not it was tuberculosis. It was a negative or positive test.

I nearly fainted! I had to lean on the back of a chair to hold myself up. I was so mad that I hadn't been told! Again, I turned to my mother and said, "Why didn't you tell me then, instead of waiting until the night before we leave to go there? Does anybody else know? She said "Yes, I had to tell the principal so they might contact everyone you have come in contact with in the last 6 weeks. I told some people downtown where you frequently go to hang out. I contacted all your friend's parents and the church members. I told them you did not know and not to tell you if they saw you." By this time the tears were running down my face and I was not able to control them. Memories of my 3- month isolation with tuberculosis at the age of 5 came pouring back into my memory. I prayed this was not a repeat.

She told me they were going to take my convertible and park it in the implement business until I came back. She told me I needed to pack plenty of pajamas and clothes that I wanted to wear daily because I would be able to dress daily. Her words were flowing right over my head as I was devastated. Daddy had sat through this whole drama without saying a word. He looked as though he was going to cry, too Neither of them had attempted to hug me or console me in any way. They had never been kissers or huggers so I was not surprised. I walked over and sat down by Daddy, and he reached over and held my hand. He squeezed my hand tight and said "Lydia, you are going to have to be strong because this is something we cannot help you with." I said, "I know, but at least I could have been told so that I might say good-by to my friends and Aunt Ann and Uncle Billy." Mother said, "Aunt Ann and Uncle Billy are coming in the morning before we plan to leave to tell you good-bye."

I turned to mother and said, "Why would you do this to me? I have noticed people staring at me this week, and some appeared to be talking about me. You have given me no chance to tell my friends good-bye and have alienated the people I know, because they are all fearful of me now."

Then I really became mean and angry saying to Mother "It's just like you to suck all the sympathy from the town toward you. All my life you've wanted them to praise you for what a wonderful mother you are. I think you're delighted to see me go! At the moment, I don't see anyone in this room crying except Daddy and me." I could tell it shocked her because I had never talked back to her. With that I went to my room and closed the door. I got my clothes out to start packing. I wasn't sure what I could or could not take. I could not focus on the packing job because of all the terrible things going through my head. I laid down in my clothes and cried myself to sleep. I awakened about 1am to another sleepless night. All my dreams for the future were collapsing, as my mind ran from one bad spot to another of what might happen and when. Why me, Lord?

The next morning as we were preparing to leave, a boy named

Steven that I had just started dating came to see me. He said he wanted to take the long trip to the Sanatorium with me. I had mixed feelings about this as I had already exposed him to the disease. If it came back positive after the test. I would really feel guilty. I told him that, but he said he didn't care, because he had already been exposed and taken the test like everyone else in town and was negative. He said he wanted go along, if I would allow him to join me. I didn't answer, but he came anyway. Daddy told me good-by and gave me one of those rare hugs, then the three of us started the long journey to a new episode in my life.

As we traveled down the road to my destination, I thought of Mother driving Daddy through the snow storm in the 1940's attempting to get to the sanatorium so they might save his life. How much their devotion to each other had changed since then! He was still as much in love with her as he had always been. I didn't know how she really felt about him. She still continued her infidelity and he acted as though nothing was wrong. She also used to act as though nothing was wrong when he was an alcoholic. He had been sober, now for 7 years, but they had never been able to be a real couple again (at least they never showed it in front of me). He slept in one room and she slept in another. Mother's threat of divorce was after they reconciled in 1953. She had proclaimed that she would stay until I left for college or left home. That threat should be coming to a head right now. Nothing had been said.

My thoughts were interrupted by the young man named Steven who rode with me. I was sitting in the front seat and he was in the back. Steven said, "How long will you have to stay over here?" I said, "I don't know a thing about this. I just found out I was going last night. Ask Mother." Mother said "I understood they will run a sputum test and it will take six weeks to get the result back. If the results are negative, you can come back home and get ready to go to college. If they come back positive, you will have to have a second six- week test, then stay until it comes back negative." I'm sitting their figuring in my mind how long we are talking about. This was the first week of June, so I might be out by the middle of July. If not, I would still be out by the last of August hopefully in time to start school late. I've always been an optimist. We'd have to wait and see how this played out.

CHAPTER 28

THE SANATORIUM

I had been to the sanatorium when I was a child, and my dad had been a patient there. This hospital was a state hospital that specialized in Tuberculosis (also known as the White Plague), histoplasmosis and any other lung problems. A lot of people think that TB is only of the lung. You can have it in other parts of the body such as the kidneys, liver, fluid surrounding the brain and spinal cord, heart muscles, genitals, lymph nodes, bones, joints, skin, walls of blood vessels and voice box.

Built in 1907, and covering 60 acres, it had its own farm fields, dairy cows, barns, fire department, water tower, laundry, hot house and power house. It sat at the highest point in Missouri overlooking the town below. Although this was a state hospital, it was open to anyone financially able to be treated there. Private pay did not entitle you to any better bedding arrangements. It was the best treatment you could receive in the state and attracted people with money. They had a large number of doctors who were from all over the world. Most of the countries they were from had a lot of tuberculosis patients. They were there to learn how to more effectively treat the disease.

As we drove onto the grounds, it looked like a college

campus. The grounds were immaculate! The administration and registration building were red brick with white columns. There was a red brick wing attached to each side of the main building. Behind this beautiful façade was the infirmary where entering patients had their beds in long narrow rooms. The patients were facing windows from one end to the other of what they called a veranda. There were two beds placed against each side of a partition high enough that the patients could not see each other. The purpose was to keep them from breathing one another's germs. Behind the beds was a long room with bathrooms and showers. A small sitting area was available when a guest came to see you so that you might have some privacy. That room had windows all around so that privacy was limited to conversation only, as everyone could see you.

The facility had a total of 12 buildings placed in the form of a Maltese cross. Eight of the buildings housed patients and the others were used for support services. The patient's buildings had four verandas with eight to ten beds on each one. The Gupton and the Schaffler were men's housing. The Minor and the Dusenburg, were the women's housing. The year that I was there was 1961, the year that integration took hold so they moved the black people out of what had been the Baker building, shared by men and women, into the other facilities with the whites. Each building had a large dining room and a common area room off each veranda, for sharing one small black and white television. Tables were set up for puzzles, games and cards. There were a few small private rooms on each veranda. They were for long term residences. One of the ladies there had a private room for 7 years. One of the other buildings used for support services was used to house men and women from the state penitentiary. Patients from mental facilities were put in with the regular patients, unless they were dangerous. A second building was used to house the nurses.

Mother wasted no time in getting me registered. Steven unloaded the things I had brought and carried them into the veranda. This was the last I saw of him because they would not let him come into the women's area. I looked down the veranda and it seemed endless. I turned around, hugged Steven good-bye as well as thanked him for coming. Everyone was interested in seeing the new patient, as they all quit doing what they had been involved in, and stared at the newcomer. My heart sank because everyone I saw was as old as my mother or older (or so I thought). Many of them had not combed their hair and hardly any had make-up on. They all had on pajamas and house slippers except for a few casually clothed in loose fitting garments.

We had walked almost to the other end when we came upon an empty bed. Across the partition, in the next bed was a young woman in her early 20's. She smiled and looked happy to see me. She said, "Hi, I'm Cheryl, what's your name?" and I said, "Lydia". She said, "Are you from the city?" and I said, "No, I live on a farm." She said," I'm surprised, you're dressed like a city person. I live on the farm also. I'm excited to see you, as most of the people on this veranda are from the city or a small town. At least we'll have something in common to talk about. You're going to share the partition with me. Welcome!"

Mother interrupted Cheryl's conversation to tell me that she and Steven needed to get started back. The nurses and house-keepers at the infirmary were standing there wanting to help me settle in. Mother said she would be back to see me later. She had given me some money to make a phone call if I needed anything, "Otherwise, she said, "I will write you and Aunt Ann will also." She kissed me on the cheek and turned and walked out.

CHAPTER 29

ON MY OWN

I turned to the nurse and told her I needed to go to the restroom first. She showed me where to go. As I was coming out of the restroom, I turned the wrong direction and stepped into a hall. Before I could turn around, a man who looked like a policeman, walked by with a woman in handcuffs and shackled feet. He stepped between her and me. She glared at me and shuffled on down the aisle. The nurse yelled at me that the area I had stepped in was off limits and said to come with her. On the way back to my bed, I asked the nurse why the woman was in the handcuffs and she said, "Like you, she arrived today but at the women's prison. She just finished with some tests. She is going to her cell in one of the other buildings." I said, "What did she do wrong?" The nurse said, "She murdered someone and most likely has picked up tuberculosis in the prison where she was. The only time you will see her out again is for tests or the monthly movie. You might never see her again if she doesn't conform to the rules. Do not attempt to visit with any of the prisoners, nor get close to them." I did not particularly want to see her again as the look in her eyes was very scary.

We returned to my bed. The nurse opened my suitcase and

dumped everything on the bed. There laid all the luxury clothing items that I had received for graduation, plus a box of monogrammed stationary. She said, "These silk things are not going to do well here, as everything you own has to be placed in boiling water to eliminate the germs. Neither you or your mother apparently read the list of things you should bring. I will get you some cotton pajamas for today, but you must call your mother to have her send three pairs. You will wear each pair for a week. You must have one to wear, one in the drawer under the bed and one in the wash. There are towels and wash clothes in the bathroom closet for you to use. Do not use anyone else's or let them use yours. The soap is on a shelf, in the shower, there are no bathtubs. All your personal belongings are placed under your bed. All the meals are served to you on a tray, and we change the beds. Any feminine pads you will have to provide yourself. You are not allowed to step out of this building for any reason, unless you are with a nurse or other personnel. Do you understand?" I said "Yes."

When I was in the rest- room I had noticed that the towels, wash clothes, and soap were stamped with the initials "MSP". I asked her what the initials stood for. She said, "Missouri State Penitentiary." "They make all our items and get paid a minimal fee for it. The blankets on the bed are also stamped. If you need a mild soap for your face, you better have your mother send some, as the soap they make is much like "lye" soap and hard on the skin." I knew what my first call home was going to be about. I was waiting until the next day to see if there were any more surprises before I wrote it. I changed into my loaned cotton pajamas and sat down on the bed next to Cheryl. I said, "How long have you been here?" She said, "A little over two weeks. I work in a medical facility and must have picked up the germ from someone there. I am engaged to a man that is getting ready to be drafted because of the problems in a place called Vietnam. I am hoping to be back home after four more weeks are up, and my test comes back. I'm a Catholic, and I brought my Rosary. I pray it every night, asking that I will be released, so I may see him before he leaves." I said I don't know about Rosaries. She said, "If you would like, I will show you tonight before "Lights out". I said, "I would like that."

I lived in a community where there were only Protestant churches and had only been inside a Catholic Church once in my life. I laughed when I thought of that visit and I could remember vividly what happened 7 years ago. This Rosary would be my second introduction to what Catholics believed.

My Aunt Ann had taken me to a beautiful Catholic Church in a small town nearby to attend the 8th Grade graduation of an older cousin of mine. I was about 10 years old at the time and was awed by the beautiful stain glass windows and statues I observed on the way to my seat. Aunt Ann let me sit on the aisle so I could see better. She had also cautioned me not to say a word while we were in there. I had seen all the girls dressed in their white dresses and the boys in their black suits all lined up while waiting to parade down the aisle. I knew this was going to be special!

The Procession began, and the bishop was in attendance to perform the ceremony. When I saw him in the beautiful attire used for these occasions, I was stunned and loved every minute. As they progressed into the mass, they handed him what I would later learn was incense. I did not see the lighting of the incense, but did see the smoke rising from it. I thought, "Oh, my goodness, his beautiful clothes must be on fire. I turned in my seat and looked at all the others sitting around me. I thought, "What's wrong with these people?" No one else seemed to notice, and I was anticipating yelling "Fire" but had been cautioned by Aunt Ann not to say a word. I decided that first I'd lean out to get a better look. The edge of the pew was very shallow so I lost my balance, then I fell into the aisle!

I never knew my aunt could be so fast! She reached out with

one hand and grabbed the tail of my dress and drug me back into the pew. I could tell by her expression she was not pleased. Everyone around us had turned to look as I was restored to my seat. I sat upright in the pew afraid I would miss something else, but everything seemed fine, and I saw the bishop waving the incense ball around. Now, I was totally confused about the fire and the smoke. I could not wait to talk to Aunt Ann about it. She looked "cross" so I waited until we got in the car and closed the door.

She said, "What in the world were you doing in there?" I explained to her what I thought was going on and she burst out laughing. She said "I'm just glad you didn't get the opportunity to yell "Fire."

Those thoughts dissipated as they rang the bell for dinner. We returned to our beds, waiting on our food trays to come. Then two older, friendly ladies next to us started a conversation. They were very interested in how I gotten the disease, and before dinner was over, they had accepted me into their "Circle."

Tuberculosis during the 1950's and 1960's mostly infected people that lived in poverty, or those in prisons or institutions where occupants were crowded. In the poverty situation, malnutrition, poor health practices and lack of proper medical attention was the reason most people 's immune systems broke down which allowed the germ to enter their bodies. In my case, there been three generations of the disease. The oldest generation of our family had died because there was no treatment for it, other than moving to a dry climate. This might have prolonged the disease but did not stop it. The next generation was fortunate to have the use of streptomycin shots and surgical removal of diseased tissue. I was treated with Streptomycin and isolation the first time I had it in 1948 at the age of 5. No surgery was required. Now I was to be treated with eight PAS pills and one INH pill, a total of 27, three times a day.

The first morning I was there, they gave me my nine- pill

breakfast. I was sitting there swallowing one at a time, when the nurse said, "You're going to get tired of that, so let me teach you to swallow them all at once. She said put all of them in your mouth then move them to the back of your throat. Take a four-ounce glass of water, tilt it up to send the water to the back of your throat and swallow at the same time. If you don't succeed the first time, practice each time you take your pills until you do. Just remember to relax your throat." A day later I could do it.

They took me for a chest x-ray and showed me the lesion on my right lung. It was the size of an eraser on a pencil. I was amazed they had found it. Next, they took me to a very white, sterile looking room where a nurse was putting on gloves in anticipation of giving me what was called a "gastric." I was not advanced enough in my disease to cough up sputum. Those who could spit up sputum had it placed in a petri dish or some other container for growth. Then they would let it grow for six weeks. This would either come back positive or negative and that determined your stay time. Since I did not produce sputum, they would take a pointed tube, which they would push up my nose, and down my throat into my stomach. They would draw out a specific amount of liquid for the test. This was very uncomfortable so they would try to do it as quickly as possible, without gagging you. I hated it and hoped this would be the only one I ever had done. Then I returned to the infirmary to find a lady waiting to take me to another test.

They took me into a very nice room to someone who I assumed was a psychologist. She told me she was to evaluate me so that I might be properly placed, should I have to stay. She was surprised at how healthy I appeared to be, and that my attitude was optimistic. She had my records from school as well as what seemed like my life history. I was suspect that she had gotten this information from my mother during the few days after the original diagnosis. Mother had three days after she found out the diagnosis to get this information together, during the time that I was oblivious to my health problem. She commended me on my good grades from high school. She asked me if I would be interested in taking some college courses from a local university. I was excited and said, "Yes." She said, "Later in your stay they will give you an IQ test. Then someone from the university will be available to discuss what courses you might take. I would be limited to a "small time frame" as it was imperative that I rest twice a day and at night.

Back to the infirmary to rest before lunch. I decided while lying there, unable to sleep, that I would walk around that afternoon introducing myself to the other 26 ladies on the veranda. Not all of them were happy to meet me. Some were shy and introverted, some were just not social, and some were depressed because of their health problems. Others were just like Cheryl and me, just trying to be cordial until the culture came back, which would determine whether we went home or stayed.

Mail time was an exciting part of the day. Friends and relatives from home would write me letters, to keep me up to date on what everyone was doing. The local weekly newspapers would send me a newspaper every week. It was treasured not only be me but by others who had no access to any newspapers. There were some letters that I didn't enjoy.

One of the letters was from the man with the big cheeks that stalked me in high school. He was still in the army and had finally ceased writing mother letters about me. As I said before, he didn't know what the word punctuation meant, nor could he spell. He still did not put a period at the end of a sentence or capitalize "I". His time in the army had not been used to educate him. It was difficult to decipher what all the words, many of which were misspelled and were running together meant. The point of the letter was very insulting to me. He said that he was willing now to accept me as his girlfriend, because no one else would want me now that I had tuberculosis. He went on to say he was also willing to marry me, then as soon as he came home from the army, he would make those arrangements. Needless to say, I did not write him back.

I think some people don't know what to say in this unusual situation I was experiencing. While others were just cruel. For instance, one person wrote to tell me that she knew the real reason I had left town. She and her friends had decided that I was pregnant and had gone off to have a baby. She knew when I came home that the child was probably going to be put up for adoption, but if I decided to keep the baby there was no shame in that. She stated that she would always be my friend and that I could confide in her when I had no one else. This girl was only an acquaintance, and I think she was trying to spread gossip about me. I wrote her back and sent it in a Sanatorium envelope that I had requested from one of the nurses. When I asked the nurse for it, I told her the reason. She was very sympathetic and said, "As if you don't have enough problems. I find it sad that someone proclaiming to be your friend would do that to you." I told her she had never been a friend, nor would she ever be now. I never heard from the girl again after I wrote her back.

The weeks dragged on by, and the time was getting closer for the results of the cultures to come back. Two weeks before Cheryl's culture came back, a woman directly across from me was moved to one of the "women's out buildings" as her culture was positive. She had been pretty sick and starting to cough up blood, so she was not surprised. Everyone told her good bye and wished her luck. It was a sad moment for her and everyone concerned. We were not allowed to touch each other, and she looked as though she needed a good hug. We all gathered around her. It was a melancholy group that stood there. Foremost in everyone's mind was, "Will this be me when the culture comes back?" Far more patients stayed than were released when that day came. The cleaning crew cleaned up the vacated space and disinfected it. We wondered how long it would be before someone took her place.

The next morning, we found out. Here was the new girl and

she was no older than me. Oddly, she had no one with her. She had coal black hair that was coarse and straight. She had a pretty face, a body frame that was very thin, but her attitude was sullen. The nurses went through the routine of explaining everything. She never said a word or asked any questions. When the nurse was finished, and they emptied the contents of her bag, the things she owned were very meager. Cheryl and I were eager to get acquainted, but when we said hello, she nodded her head and turned away. After everything was finished, she changed into the one pair of pajamas she had brought, she climbed into her bed and turned her back to both of us.

Right before "lights out" Cheryl got out her Rosary, expressed her request, which was that she would have her culture come back negative. Then, she and her fiancé could be married before he left for service. I expressed my request, which was that I would have a negative culture, and be able to start to college this semester. We had said the Rosary faithfully for 4 weeks now. I could say it just like she could and no longer needed the instructions on the sheet of paper she had written for me. Out of the corner of my eye, I could see the new girl peeking, trying to see what we were doing. Not a word was said, as we completed the Rosary. Cheryl put it away, kissed the picture of her fiancé goodnight and we waited for the lights to go off

On the new girl's second morning there, she was sound asleep when the breakfast call came. The nurse came in and told her she was to wake up, go to the restroom and wash her hands for breakfast. When she returned, I said, "My name is Lydia and I would like to know your name if you and I are going to be bedmates," and I smiled. She said, "I'm Arlene and I don't want to make friends. I just want to go home." I said, "I would like to go home too, but we need to find out if we're well enough to go home, first. You could be my part time friend until you go home." She smiled. I asked her where she was from and the town was only 45 miles from where I had lived. She had graduated high school and was working two jobs to try to help her older sister become a nurse. Once she became a nurse, she was going to help Arlene get an education in whatever she wanted to do. She said she had been working these jobs since she was a junior in high school. She guessed she wasn't getting enough rest to keep her healthy. One of the jobs required a TB test, which she had failed. Cheryl joined the conversation, and we all began to get acquainted. Arlene also felt she was letting her sister down, as she only lacked one year of school being finished.

Arlene was offered the same opportunity as me to take the college courses but refused. I later believed she did not have the money for them as she was not a "Paid Patient" but instead a "state patient." Two weeks after she arrived, Cheryl's test came back and she was called to the office. Arlene and I waited anxiously for her results. When she came back in the door, she was excited. She was negative! She was going home! All those Rosary recitations had paid off! We were both very happy for her, but blue because we would miss her. She called her family, and they arrived before dark to pick her up. This meant that only two weeks were left before my results would be back.

Those two weeks were some of the longest I have ever experienced. Arlene and I played games and cards and watched the one tv when there was something on that we liked. When 30 people are sharing the same TV it is hard to get an agreement on what to watch. The day before the test results, I was sent for another X-ray. I hoped it was my last one here.

Finally, the day came and the night before, I could not sleep. Arlene and I were whispering back and forth while the other patients were telling us to be quiet. Then someone told on us, causing the nurse to come out and lecture us about how important rest was. I finally drifted off to sleep.

The next thing I remember is waking up to a beautiful sun shiny day. I laid there thinking surely nothing can go wrong on a day like today. I said a prayer that I might be released today.

Going through my mind were all the things I needed to do to get ready to go to college. One of those things was to replace the silk-monogramed pajamas they had boiled and ruined the day I came here.

They brought our breakfast, and I could see that Arlene was not happy. I said, "What's wrong?" She said, "I don't know what I'm going to do by myself here. You're the only friend I have and there is no one else here my age." I said, "it won't be long until your test will be back and you'll probably be going home. Besides there is no guarantee that I'll be negative, either." Arlene said, "Everyone here says you act and look so healthy, they're sure you will be negative." I said, "I hope so."

An hour later, they called me to come to the main office. When I sat down in the chair, I was so nervous that my legs were shaking. My doctor came in and he had a strong foreign accent. He took out an X-ray from a folder and placed it on a screen so that we both might see it. He said "The chest X-ray looks really good, as I can hardly see the small lesion that you had when you came in here 6 weeks ago. I wish that the lesion was all we had to worry about as your TB culture came back positive. Because of the culture, you will have to have another six weeks test. To further complicate matters, the State of Missouri Board of Health has just this month decided that anyone with TB, in a hospital environment must have 6 months of negative reports, before they may be released back into the public. So, if all your upcoming tests are negative, you will be able to be released in January of 1962. Normally, you would be released after the next six- week test, if it was negative. This new law is trying to help cut down on the number of people who leave here when they are not truly healed. They don't take their medicine properly after they get home, and end up carrying their disease back to their family. Shortly after that, we have additional patients from that same family. We also have the problem of people who just walk off and disappear. They infect several others in the public. If this continues, we will be like a "Third World Country" and will have lost control of the disease completely. Because of the large number of patients this facility has, the authorities have decided to put up a fence around the hospitals to control loss of patients."

My brain was spinning trying to grasp all the information my doctor is telling me. My thoughts were keeping me from hearing anything else he had to say. He said again, "Do you understand? Are you listening?" I was so choked up I could not respond. He said, "I have sent the results to your parents. You may call them after this meeting if you wish." He handed me a letter regarding this conversation, and I tried to stand up. I could not make myself come upright and sank back into the chair. He said, "Let me help you up. Lydia, you are young and have a lot of life in front of you. It's not the end of the world." He opened the door and led me outside to where the phone was, then shut the door behind me. I did not want to call my parents. What could they do? I did not want a lecture on being strong and how tough they knew I was. I wanted someone to hold me, then tell me that this too would pass, and they would be there for me until that time came. There was no one there for that, no siblings, no friends, and certainly no one else closer than 500 miles away who cared.

I was standing on my feet, walking back to my room, unable to control my emotions. I wanted to scream! I walked up to my bed in the infirmary, turned and looked at Arlene. She said, "What did you find out? Are you negative?" I couldn't talk! I handed her the paper he had given me and walked into the bathroom. I went to the very last stall and I started crying. I sobbed and sobbed until my nose hurt and my head was totally stopped up, and I could not hear good. I sat down on the commode because I felt so weak. I looked at the prison soap and the towels with the prison logo and thought about the fact, I would be fenced in like the prisoners that resided in the other building. I said out loud, "Lord what have I done to deserve this? Was it my vanity? Are you trying to teach me to be humble? All these people here with me have nothing, when I thought I had everything. Now we are all on the same level. Perhaps this is a lesson in humility?"

After an hour long "pity party" I tried to be rational and figure out how I was going to make it until 1962. I looked in the mirror and said to myself, "I can be stronger than this and I will figure out how to make time pass quickly. Hopefully I could do something worthwhile with my time." I was weak from the crying, so I poured warm water over my prison wash-cloth to wash my face. It didn't help much as my eyes and nose were swollen and I looked awful. I started throwing cold water on my face which helped a little. I could make the outside look better, but it was going to take a lot longer to make the inside heal.

When I got back to my bed the letter was laying there. Arlene said, "I'm so sorry" and I said, "I know." The Sanatorium printed a newsletter monthly which was due the next week. No one knew except Arlene and me about the extra 6 months we all were going to have to stay, or about the new fence enclosure. I did not tell anyone except Arlene, as I was the only patient for test results that day, and I did not know if it was public knowledge or not. I received the piece of paper regarding my release and the change but wondered if the doctor had given it to me by mistake.

That night I was not interested in conversation, but almost everyone on the floor came by to tell me how sorry they were. I looked at them and thought, "These are women at all stages of waiting for the results of their tests, some 1 week, all the way through to 6 weeks for others. None of them know what I do about the change in their life that is about to occur. This is like a prisoner waiting for a parole and now instead of the time being decreased for good behavior, it is increased through no fault of their own. What misery this is going to create for mothers that are wanting to go home to their families with small children. For older women, whose life has been shortened by this disease already, this is going to take away 6 more precious months of what life they have left."

The fence would start construct on that same week. The newsletter was delivered to the patients the same day the fencing materials were unloaded. It was almost like a revolution in the infirmary and out buildings! The men were twice as vocal as the women regarding the extra time added onto our "sentences." There were plenty of tears shed in the infirmary, and I'm sure most of the out buildings regarding this intrusion into their lives. The fence was an insult to all of us, as the people trying to escape were few and far between. Some of the mental patients didn't understand about the fence and became very unsettled and scared. It was the topic of conversation for several days without any satisfactory response to our questions and concerns by the administration.

The next morning there stood the nurse with a transportation cart to collect my things. I looked at Arlene and could tell she was going to be stoic and quiet again. I told her they were moving me to one of the women's out buildings called The Minor. If she had to stay it would be 4 more weeks before her test was back. Maybe, she would get to go home. If not, there was no guarantee that she would be put in the same building with me. We both should ask for the Minor building if she had to stay. The Minor had verandas on every side. There were usually 8 beds on each one. Now I was going to be living with 7 strangers and have to get acquainted all over again. There was a whole row of windows that the beds faced. Those windows had huge awnings all the way across the outside of the room. On each side of the building was a veranda, a total of 4 plus some private rooms, in the center of the building where long term and bedfast patients lived. Upstairs was two rooms with two patients in each room. These were coveted rooms as these patients had one full bath that the four of them shared. The view from upstairs was beautiful looking across the hillsides into the small quaint town below.

Unlike the infirmary, the outbuildings didn't have as much heat in the winter, no air conditioning, but fans in the summer, and the windows were left open every night. They still were using the concept developed in 1907 which said "fresh air, sunshine, nutrition and bed rest." They said if you closed the windows at night, you would be inviting infection from your bed mates. There was no partition between the beds.

Leaving the windows open at night was unpleasant with the heat. The humidity wasn't as bad as it had been in my hometown where a swamp was reclaimed for farmland. The swamp was gone, but not the humidity. Fortunately, the Sanatorium was on one of the highest elevations in the state, which made it some-what cooler.

I was assigned a bed between two women. The one on my right, a grandmother was very friendly and had a great sense of humor. The one on my left was a young mother probably in her mid to late twenties. The grandmother, whose name was Martha, told me that she had tuberculosis of the kidney and had been there for over a year. The attractive young mother, named June said she had been there for 10 months and counted the days until she was to be released. Now she had found out that she was having a longer stay like everyone else. She was tearful when she told me that she developed the disease right after the birth of her first child. Two months after the birth she discovered she had TB and was placed here in the Sanatorium. Her daughter was now having her 1st birthday this week-end, and her husband was bringing the baby to see her mother. Tears ran down her face, as she told me she had not been allowed to see her except through a window, nor hold her since she had come here. She said, "I have missed all of her babyhood because of this disease. She doesn't even know who I am when she sees me. I worry that we will never have the bond of mother and child since she has been raised by another." I told her how sorry I was and hoped that they would all enjoy the first birthday party. I sat up in bed and introduced myself to the rest of the ladies, then thought how I was more fortunate than I realized.

At the far end of the veranda and against the wall was the last bed. It was occupied by an overweight woman about 40. She had pictures of dogs and kittens taped all over the wall and behind the bed. Everyone there, except for her, told me their name and their story. She was quiet and sitting up in the bed hugging her knees and rocking. Martha turned to me and said, "That is Sally. She was brought here by the State Home for the Feeble-minded. She has the IQ of a 5- year- old. You never know what she is going to say. Rarely is it rational." I said, "Hello Sally," and she cocked her head and looked at me. I said, "I'm Lydia and I like dogs and cats, too." She turned around and looked at me and said. "Do you like kitties and puppies?" I said, "Yes, and you have so many pretty pictures of them." She smiled, then went back to rocking in the bed.

Martha also told me that when Sally had her period every month, she would think she was dying. She warned me that she would be screaming and crying about all the blood and dying. It would take the nurses an hour or so to calm her down and clean her up, then try to teach her about how to use the pads to stop the blood. She would be fine for the next few days and when the next month came, it would all be forgotten again and they would have to repeat the whole process.

The mental patients had all been integrated into each veranda. Some had two. I was walking around through all the verandas, just trying to get acquainted with everyone and could easily pick the mental patients out. Some were friendly, some were not. We all were eating in a common dining room here instead of on a bed tray like the infirmary. I would see all these people every day and would know all their names before I was released. The good news was the veranda had its own TV for only 8 people, instead of 30 so it was a little easier to watch some programs you enjoyed.

In between were the private rooms reserved for people with long term recovery problems. I stopped in the doorway to visit in one room. I was not invited in. The lady sitting in the bed had a very beautiful face. Her hair was a pretty shade of grey and she had it pulled into a neat bun and her eyes were hazel. She must have been about 65 years old. I introduced myself and told her my story. She smiled, then said "I have been here the longest of any resident. I have tuberculosis of the blood and have been here 7 years. I am getting better, but several times I have improved only to have the disease reestablish itself again. I was a professor at a university nearby for my whole career. I will tell you, the hardest part of being here is being bored. Do you play chess?"

I told her I had not played chess, but I was willing to learn. Her face brightened up! "You're the first person to tell me that. During our free time, perhaps you could come here and I will teach you. You must wear a mask and wash your hands before you touch the chess pieces. You have a fresh, active case of TB, and I can't take any chances." I said I would and so began my introduction to chess.

Mother called. She said she had the letter about my having to stay. She also told me that she and Daddy were coming to see me on Sunday. She asked me how I was and I said, "Fine." She didn't say, "I'm sorry, I know you're upset, or we love you and hate you're having to go through this, or anything consoling." I wondered how long she had known. I had found out on Monday and moved Tuesday. This is Friday but she didn't say when she got the letter. Nothing from Daddy. The visit on Sunday started when they arrived at noon. We sat outside on the bench near the front door. They were not allowed to touch me and had to wear masks. Daddy said he couldn't believe the new restrictions about leaving nor could he believe they were building the fence. Mother visited with me about the pajamas and other items she had brought me. Most were small gifts of candy, cookies and other things that friends and neighbors had sent. She also told me that all the tuberculin tests, performed on boys and girls, I went to school with had all come back negative. She stood up abruptly and walked over to some other patients and started a conversation. She did not return to where I was until it was time to leave an hour later.

Daddy and I talked about different subjects and laughed about some of the things my friends and I did when I was a teenager at home. Then he talked to me about what I should do to be careful in the hospital. His experience of being there had given him lots of pointers on how to keep from getting a new infection from some of the other patients. I listened and agreed with him. Some things I had never thought of before. Mother came over and said it was time to leave." I'll see you soon", she said. Daddy stood up and blew me a kiss and they left. I missed Arlene, and I was wondering how she was today. It was visitor time and no one ever came to see her. I never knew if her family was unable to make the trip or not. She received little mail and never talked about it. A lot of the patients that were state patients never had company. I don't know if their families lived too far away or if they could not afford the gas. Regardless, it was sad for those families not to be together.

I started back in the building when I noticed June, the young mother and her husband with the birthday baby. They were standing by his car. He had brought a camera and was taking pictures of June and wanted to take a picture of her and the baby together. She couldn't touch the child so he reached in the car and brought out a potty chair he had bought for the child's birthday. He propped the baby up in the potty chair and had June kneel down by her and took the picture. (I had been a photographer for the high school yearbook, so I asked if I could take a picture of the whole family.) She said she would love it and the husband picked up the baby to stand next to June. They all looked happy. Later June told me that she had laughed when she saw the potty chair as a gift. She was expecting a doll or toy for the birthday. He said, "The baby doesn't know the difference and we need the potty chair." I wished that she could have held the baby for the picture, but she knew how important it was not to pass her disease onto her child. She would smile and wave until the left, then she would go back to her bed and cry as though her heart was broken. No one ever tried to console her because this seemed to be a "ritual" for her, and the tears helped her to survive and start preparations for the next visit.

My college courses were ready to start, so my routine at the out building had to be changed. I had to be able to find time to attend on Monday, Wednesday and Friday. There were a few older people who participated. You had to be able to pay the tuition as nothing was totally free. The Sanatorium had craft classes, such as leather tooling to make purses, billfolds, belts and other leather items. I decided to take the class to make gifts for my family for Christmas. You use a swivel knife to outline patterns and other punch type tools that you struck with a mallet to make your designs. It was fun and looked very professionally done. Sewing classes and crafts were offered for entertainment and were a lot less expensive.

Every day we had to rest after lunch. You were supposed to take a nap. I have never been able to nap in the daytime. We had a fabulous library collection that was brought to us every few days. I would read a book during my naptime and had to make sure I didn't get caught because it was against the rules.

I had been asked if I would mind helping set up the auditorium for church services on Sunday morning. I would set up the Catholic Mass, get their songbooks and Missals set out, and anything else the priest might ask for. I sat in the back and attended the service. I did not know Latin so I really had no clue what was being said. As soon as they finished, I would put up the Catholic items and set out the Protestants songbooks and programs. Once again, I would sit in the back and watch the service. As soon as they finished, I would put up everything and return to my veranda. Sundays were the only day that we were free to do as we pleased, with only a short rest period in the afternoon, before the visitors came. There was no rest period required in the morning.

I also became the reporter for the newspaper that they published in house. I represented the Minor Building and interviewed all my patient inmates for "tidbits" that would interest the people in the other facilities. We all saw each other on special occasions or at the movies so this gave us a common bond. It also helped the time move faster until I could go home.

There was a once monthly group of new nurses that were brought to the Sanatorium to learn about the disease and what types of people were infected, how they coped with the stringent requirements of the hospital, and what they did that caused them to be infected. They appointed a panel to be present to take the questions from the audience. I was asked to be on the panel every month. I was told I was asked because I was a well- nourished patient from an educated household and a paid patient. There were 4 of us on the panel, 2 men, 2 women. One person was from the city, one from the farm, one from an impoverished area and me (from a small town). It was interesting to hear what the different groups asked of us.

The woman from the impoverished area was from the other women's building. She told stories of her life that made me realize that I was really an oddity here. She told of starvation when her husband left her. She did not have a job, as most women in this period of time did not work when they were stay at home mothers, with two small children. What food she could get was from neighbors as she had no family. She had considered taking up prostitution to make enough to feed her family. The food supply had gotten so scarce that she had started going through the garbage bins behind restaurants. Most of what she found, she fed to her children. She had lost more than 40 pounds and was very emaciated when she started coughing up blood. Her landlord told her she was 6 months behind on her rent, and he was going to have her evicted. She had a bad coughing spell while he was talking to her, and when he saw the blood, he called an ambulance. She ended up here and her children were checked for tuberculosis. Both had the disease. They had been put in another facility for children. She said she did not know how or when she might ever see them again. The Sanatorium did not have child patients that I knew about.

We would tell these stories to every one of the groups that attended the panel program. One man would tell his story about living homeless, without proper food, so he shoplifted and stole food and other items to sell, was arrested and thrown in jail. That was when they found out he had the disease. The other man was a paid patient with a very successful business who worked late hours, skipped meals and did not take care of himself and ended up with the disease. Now his business was suffering because of his absence. My story sounded like what it was, the story of a teenager who had what they thought was a normal life after 11 years of turmoil. My story was about tuberculosis that had covering several generations of family members. Some had died and some had lived after surgery or isolation treatment. We were what they called predisposed. In that situation, any small thing can trigger a new infection because the germ that was in my parent's body, was also in mine when they tested me for TB. It was just in an inactive state until I developed the insomnia problem, after being weakened by the Asian Flu, a few years before. Also, I did not take care of myself properly.

After listening to the plight of my other panel members, I was cautious about what I told about myself. I had just become accepted into this new environment a few weeks ago. I was living in the same quarters with them, wearing the same pajamas, sharing the living space and eating the same meals.

I certainly did not want to tell them that I was an only child who had planned to go to a private girl's college this fall, or that I had a new convertible that was parked in my father's business building until I returned. They would not have understood about my anguish of having my silk monogramed pajamas, ruined the first week, because the laundry had to boil them to kill the germs. I didn't want them to know I had expensive clothes, lived in a nice home and had anything I wanted to eat. Nor did they need to find out that my father gave me a checking account that I could write checks for money, whenever I wanted it and we had a gas pump, where my gas came from. I never had to pay for it. Until this point, I did not realize I was so spoiled, compared to anyone else in this women's outbuilding. I would hear women talking in the common room about their financial problems, and how hard it was for them to find someone to take care of their children, because they couldn't afford it. Many were concerned about their husbands, because of their long separation and no chance for intimacy, when they came to visit. Not even as much as a hug! I had no one dependent on me for anything!

This was when I began to grow up. I was only 18 but I was observing situations that only adults had to cope with. This was a dramatic character builder for me and had a great influence on my life! I began to develop empathy and sympathy for those I was sharing my life with. Daddy's words to me about the black people who worked our farms creeped back into my mind. He had said no one should ever look down on others because of the work they do. Every job is important, and everyone is just trying to make their way in this world. Always treat everyone the same. He mentioned people who thought they were wealthy and looked down their noses at people less fortunate. He said his experience with very wealthy people is they are usually very kind. It is often those who become quickly rich that want to impress others that become snobs. He always called them the "The Wannabes" because they wannabe wealthy and are putting on "airs" trying to impress people with their new found money. All those things he had told me finally meant something now. I wasn't getting my college education but I was getting an education in life, humility and humanity.

Arlene's tests came back a month later, and one of the workers in the dining room told me, she was positive. I asked her to tell Arlene to ask if she could come to the Minor building, since I was the only other person in her age bracket presently here. I asked my head nurse about having her moved here, and she said they probably would since one of the beds on our veranda was about to be vacated. The next day, Arlene moved into our veranda, and they moved her bed next to mine. We had a lot to catch up on, but we had to wait until Arlene adjusted to all the other women she did not know. She didn't adapt as quickly as I had, but I could tell she was happy to see me.

Once she became accustomed to her new surroundings, we enjoyed the ability to wander from veranda to veranda and meet other people. Also, as long as the weather was nice, we could sit outside on the benches in our free periods. Later in October, we experienced a turnover in some of the patients that had been there a long time. They were replaced with some unusual patients, one from my area of the state. When she walked in, it was hard to take your eyes off of her. She was 25-30 years of age and had tattoos all over her legs and arms, the side of her face and across the front of her neck above her breasts. These were not professionally done tattoos. She had used a product called "India Ink," which was dark black and another called "Peacock Blue." We found out her name was Cindy and that she loved to talk about herself. I had to ask why she had done this strange thing to her body. She explained to us that she used a needle and syringe to put the names of men all over her body. Arlene asked why and was told that these were men she had sex with. None of the "tats" looked very neat but you could tell the names. She was not particularly attractive in the face, but did have a full breast and nice figure plus a disdain for women who weren't covered with makeup and dressed on the "tacky side."

There were very few men in our lives, other than the yard help, delivery men, state prisoners that we saw at the movie theatre and the tray boys. The tray boys carried the food from the main kitchen to our dining room. In addition, tray boys would take individual trays to the rooms that housed the bedfast. The first meal we had after Cindy arrived was delivered by a tall skinny young man named Ray, who was not someone that would attract most women.

Arlene and I had sat down at our table, when Cindy slid into the only chair left without saying another word. She looked around, then turned to me and said, "What's his name?" I said "Who?" She said "The man behind you." I turned to look and it was Ray, the tray boy. I said, "That's Ray." She looked at her arm and down one leg and said, "I don't have that name." We were distracted by Arlene, who nearly choked on her food. She told me later, it made her laugh with a mouth full of food, when Cindy said that. During the meal, Cindy couldn't take her eyes off of Ray. Cindy was on another veranda, so the only time we usually saw her was at mealtime or during free time.

She went back to her room, and we went back to ours. I told Arlene I was not interested in being good friends with Cindy, as I couldn't determine if she was a prostitute, or just a nymphomaniac. Either way, I felt we should be kind to her, but not become her "best buddy". Arlene agreed. I felt that Cindy was just trying to shock us to see what our reaction would be to her radical lifestyle. I was wrong.

One of the verandas on the backside was not fully occupied and had a small hall behind it where you could see a greenhouse, full of beautiful flowers, as well as vegetables. The vegetables were used to give us fresh, nutritious meals, and the flowers were put in large vases, in all the administrative buildings. One of the ladies, named Kate, who lived on this veranda was an artist. Sometimes she would spend her free time doing watercolors of the flowers she could see from that position. She also was an alcoholic and had liquor brought in by friends, which she kept hidden on the veranda where she painted.

You went through a door and turned left to view the flowers, but if you turned right there was one more large window with a wide window sill. If the door was open, you could not see behind it. Kate had told everyone about the present flowers that were so colorful that she was working on. She said we all should come see the real ones. Her frequent trips to the veranda were probably not all artistic, although no one ever discovered where she hid the liquor.

We did not see Cindy at lunch and assumed she had already eaten before we got there. I told Arlene about the flowers, and we decided to go to look at them, before returning to our rooms. The people living on this veranda were still at lunch or possibly walking around on what free time they had left. We opened the door and stepped out to view the greenhouse. I shut the door. When I did, here was Arlene and me staring at Ray, whose pants were down around his ankles and his bare butt exposed. Cindy's pajama bottoms were laying in the floor. He had her up in the wide window sill having sex with her. She looked at us and waved as we turned to exit, as though it was an ordinary day and she was just saying hello. Ray didn't even acknowledge anyone was there. This was the first time, I had ever seen anyone performing the sex act in public. I was shocked! Arlene and I couldn't get back to our room quickly enough. We both started laughing, and I told Arlene I wondered if Ray would be spelled in Black or Peacock Blue. We made a quarter bet on the color selection and Arlene won with Black. It was on her ankle and she made sure we saw it the next time we were in the dining room.

We had been told about the danger of getting pregnant. There was no such thing as birth control pills so unless you had access to some other kind of protection, that could be a danger. If a girl with tuberculosis became pregnant, their hormones would make the tuberculosis worse, then you could expect a longer stay.

Now there were not many opportunities for men and women to get together. But some did and one girl got pregnant by a foreigner who was at the hospital. Sure enough, she had a year longer stay. To be truthful, I never saw anyone my age there, nor any age that seemed to be someone I would consider dating. Arlene pointed out to me that this was not about socializing with the opposite sex or being in love, but a matter of lust only. I thought she had a good point.

There were other kinds of romantic relations that were dangerous. One of the verandas had two gay women who got in a fight over another woman. One had tried to stab the other with a pair of scissors and they were put in separate verandas. Otherwise, most people were pretty docile and anxious to get well and go home. Fortunately, I was on one of the docile verandas.

Time was moving on and now it was fall. Halloween was coming. I wrote a note to Aunt Ann about needing a costume. (She always made me one every year when I was a child.) I told her they were having a contest and there would be a prize for the funniest, the prettiest and the most original. I had decided I would like to have a 1920's flapper dress and compete for the prettiest. I knew she would know exactly what to make as she had been a flapper in the 1920's. She had also taught me how to dance the "Charleston" when I was about 12. She told me she was making a pink satin dress and hat with white fringe. She sent me some of the material and fringe to make a tobacco pouch purse along with a rough drawing of how it should look. Everyone was excited about the Halloween party and contest. I had mother bring Arlene something to wear also in case she decided to participate, and she did become a ghost. The men's building won the "Most Original" with a laundry cart they had made into a baby buggy with an ugly baby. Some of the women had made a stroller with a "doll" in it pushed by a man who was dressed as a woman while a woman playing the part of the father.

When the finalist came up for the prettiest, there was a small band there made up of patients and they started playing the Charleston. I started dancing it, and all the nurses were upset because they thought it was way too strenuous for someone with my condition. Half way through they stopped the band and everyone applauded. I won the Prettiest. All the way back to my room, one of the nurses lectured me about how bad I was going to feel tomorrow, and how I had "set myself back," several months. I felt great so I did not comment. The next day I felt fine and life continued in its slow, monotonous way.

The only real "highlight" of the Sanatorium is their ability to get "First Run Movies." We saw previews of the newest movies before the general public ever saw them in the local theatre. They had a large multi-use auditorium where we all filed in from the outbuildings to enjoy the movie. The women all sat in one section, the men across the aisle. The patients from the state prison all sat in the back with the sexes segregated. The blacks filed in from their building and all sat together.

Occasionally, I would have visitors from home that were passing through this area and would stop to see me. After I was moved to the outbuildings, mother started coming every weekend. It was a five- hour drive so she would arrive a little after lunch on Sunday. If she brought someone with her such as Aunt Ann, Daddy or my boyfriend she had a different routine. She would walk in and bring me whatever I had written her that I needed or a gift from someone at home. She would visit about 15 minutes with me then wander out of my private area to visit with everyone else for the rest of the time. Whoever she had brought with her would stay with me. She would leave between 2 and 3 in the afternoon and start home.

If someone was not with her, she would arrive on Saturday after lunch, visit 15-30 minutes with me, visit the other patients then leave at the same time. I found out from Aunt Ann that she was spending Saturday night, somewhere on the way back, and arriving home after lunch on Sunday. She was telling Daddy that she wanted to spend more time with me, and I guess she thought I'd never find out. She also had started telling people that were strangers to her about how much land we owned, how successful she had been in business and a lot personal information that I felt I didn't want shared. I did not want her to tell anything about our financial conditions since so many of them had come from terrible poverty. I did not want them to think I thought I was "better" than they were. A few girls said something to me about things she had said, so I told them she had a bad habit of exaggerating. I never said anything else about it.

When I confronted her about this information she was giving them, she got mad. She said, "Maybe I shouldn't even come over here. It's a real effort for me to come and see you ever week, and you don't appreciate it." I said, "Why don't you just come over when someone else is coming with you instead of every week so you won't have to spend the night?" Her face got red and I could tell I had struck a nerve. I said, "This would give you more time on the week-ends to do something with Daddy instead of leaving him there by himself. You know he would not come over here to visit me without going back home the same day. The 15 to 30 minutes you spend with me is not worth the trip. Is there nothing you can talk to me about or say so that both of us could enjoy each other's company, for at least an hour? You spend an hour and a half entertaining the other people I live with telling them how wealthy you are. You have never spent that kind of time with me since I was a baby. You have always seemed to enjoy other people more than me. Daddy and I have never been as important to you as these strangers are. Is it because you can impress them? Also, I know why you are spending the night and it makes me sad, and No, I won't tell Daddy!" With that she teared up and said, "Why are you so hateful?" She stood up and nearly ran out of the room without saying good-bye. Two weeks later I received a letter from her telling me how much she loved me and that she missed me. I still have that letter. This was the first time I had ever had a proclamation of adoration from my mother.

On August 15, 1961, Grandfather Clay died. He had developed stomach cancer and had asked to come home a few years before to live with his children. He explained that he was absolutely destitute. Only two children would help him, Aunt Ann and one uncle. Mother had never forgiven him for running away to Texas with their female cousin, taking all his cash and deserting the family when she was 5 years old. Her other two brothers held a grudge also. Mother said she would not come to get me for the funeral. I had enjoyed him as he had a very interesting life, which he had enjoyed sharing with me. When I was at Aunt Ann's, I would visit him, and he would talk about living with the Indians as a child and all the wonderful things he had learned from their culture. He also told me about the oil wells he had owned that never produced, as well as all sorts of fragments of his life. The hospital had granted me a two- day pass which I wanted to use. But she didn't want to go to the funeral nor did she want to make the trip to pick me up. I was entitled to a 4 day pass the week after Christmas but those 4 months seemed so far away.

Fall came and the temperature began to drop and having the windows open at night became a problem. The mattresses on the bed were only 3 to 4 inches thick and as fall changed into winter, November and December became unbearable.

To prepare us for the winter, the nurses passed out additional prison blankets. They also gave us a flannel cap which tied under your chin to keep your head warm at night. Flannel pajamas and a heavy robe was purchased by my parents to keep me warm. Also, we had woolen socks. Arlene did not have any warm things so I asked my parents if they could bring a robe and some other warm items for her. Otherwise, she would have had lighter things, such as old faded gowns that patients who had nothing received when they arrived, or they had died and left them. These would be given to her by the Sanatorium.

By the time December came, the cold came through to you from the bottom of your mattress. I utilized the weekly newspapers sent to me from the two publishers in my home county. I put layers of them between the metal springs and the mattress to insulate it. I had learned that newspaper was insulating, long ago when I had been in a poor friend's house, where they had filled the spaces between boards with newspaper, to keep out the cold. I shared the newspapers with Arlene and everyone on the veranda. I thought this was crazy! In an attempt to keep us from breathing each other's germs, they were freezing us to death. It was a wonder that patients didn't get sicker from this fresh air method.

One night it was so cold, and the wind was blowing snow that was being "sifted" into a fine powder through the screens. Once this landed on the floor, it became very hazardous for walking. It was snowing so hard you could only see the glow of the administration buildings bright lights. You could not discern the shape of any of the other buildings around us. We could not get warm! We all stayed in the common room where the TV was as long as we could. Finally, the lights cut sent us back to the veranda. They had cleaned a path through the snow to prevent falling. We put on all our sleeping gear, then wore our robes and two pairs of socks to stave off the cold, and climbed into bed. You could hear the howling of the wind and it was making everyone shiver. The wind was whipping the bedcovers around so that you had to roll up in the covers to keep your body covered.

At the nurse's station there were hot water bottles, all in a row hanging on the back wall, and for some reason we were not allowed to have them. After asking about them and being refused access, I told Arlene to stand watch until all the nurses had gone for their "break." I climbed upon a desk chair and stole as many as I could carry. Some of the older women refused to take them as they were fearful, they would get in trouble, so I returned those back to the hooks they were on. The rest of us filled our bottles with hot water and went to bed. The warmth was wonderful!

We all had to make our own beds in the out buildings, unlike the Infirmary which functioned like an ordinary hospital. No one would know that we had the hot water bottles, because I collected them all early next morning before everyone made their beds. Arlene stood watch, and I put them all back. Apparently, no one ever noticed they were gone and none of the women on the veranda told on us.

Next morning, the orderly came, swept the snow into a large dust pan and emptied it into a bucket. I wanted to make snowballs but was not allowed to touch it. He then mopped up the wet floor and closed the windows. I could never understand why the windows could be closed in the day time, when we were still inside, but not at night. They explained to us that this method had been used since the hospital was changed by the European doctor in the 1940's. It had worked so it had never been questioned. Amazingly, no one ever got sicker from being exposed to the extreme cold.

Thanksgiving came and Christmas was not far away. Unless you had been there 6 months, you could not have a pass to go home. Arlene and I would not have been there long enough until after Christmas. Mother, Daddy, Aunt Ann and Uncle Billy could not come for Thanksgiving, so they called me. They passed the phone around and I had a nice visit with everyone including mother. I felt lonely but Arlene was lonelier than me, as no one ever came to see her and only called a few times. Her sister would occasionally write her a letter. How she felt about all this I would never know, because she never talked about it.

Every Sunday morning, they would weigh us and chart it. It was important that we build a fat reserve and keep it to fight the disease. I weighed 110 pounds and was 5'8" tall when I checked in the hospital and they were upset that I showed no gain. They insisted that I eat larger, fattier meals, and I didn't want to gain the 30 pounds that I had lost when I was 14. I started weighing in the thick red robe that mother had brought me. The nurse said, "If you're going to wear that you must wear it for every weigh-in. I did and each week would put something a little heavier in the deep pockets. They began to "rave" about how well I was doing so it worked. When I left the hospital in 1962, I weighed 6 more pounds than when I came, but 12 more in the red robe.

Every 6 weeks we had to have the sputum collected and some blood tests done. I hated it when they brought in student nurses to do this test which they called a gastric, as I still never produced any sputum. That meant they were going to take the tube, stick it up my nose and down my throat into my stomach to get the fluid for the test. A few times, it was very painful as the nursing student hadn't done it before and would hit the side going down or make my nose bleed, making the turn down into my esophagus. Once, I was sent into the test room with a new nurse that was so nervous she was shaking. I said, "Is this the first time you've done this?" She said, "Yes, I've only seen a picture of how to do it." I said, "There is no one but you and me in here. It will probably hurt me for you to try to do it and may even require more than one attempt. If you wouldn't mind, I will help you, and I will not tell on you." She looked relieved as she handed the tube to me. I stuck it up my nostril then gently make the turn to enter my throat. At this point sometimes you had to swallow over and over to get it all the way down without hitting the walls. This was one of those times. I finally got it in position for her to extract the fluid and bring it back up very slowly. She put everything together and said, "Thank you," and walked out of the room. That was the day I discovered I was not interested in the nursing field.

Right before Christmas, Mrs. Calhoun who was head nurse came in and said, "I need to talk to you and Arlene. Would you follow me to the office please?" I thought what have we done now? This nurse was not particularly fond of either of us as we were always into some mischief to relieve our boredom. This couldn't be good. Arlene and I stood inside her office and she asked us to sit down. She said, "Girls, it has come to the attention of the State that we are still segregated in this institution. We are going to move the negro women into this building and the other women's building. We will place one woman on each veranda. We are going to move the two of you into one of the semi-private rooms upstairs. In the other semi-private we are going to move two negro girls that are in your age bracket. You will have to share the bathroom. The four of you will be responsible for keeping the tub and fixtures clean. You will continue to change your own beds weekly. You can vent your windows nightly, but do not have to keep them wide open."

We were flabbergasted and excited! We did not have a TV but we did get permission to bring a radio and a record player from home. There was no common room but the bedrooms were big enough to set up a table to play games and cards. I said, "When do we move?" The answer was "Today." We gathered all our things and after a few trips up the stairs we had it all put in a closet. Later that afternoon, the two negro girls came up the stairs carrying all of their things. There was no place for personal items in the bathrooms so all of us had to keep these items in our room. We introduced ourselves to Mabry and Sasha. You could tell they were uncomfortable in this all "white" environment. They were pretty reserved and more like Arlene than me. We had no idea what was going to happen next. Once I got the record player from home then the music started, we found out. These two girls were fabulous dancers, and they proceeded to show us how to loosen up and dance. There was a small landing which connected to the hall where we would try to imitate some of their moves, and they would laugh. We all would get tickled and too loud, and one of the nurses would run up the stairs to quiet us down. It is hard to keep four teenage girls quiet.

Because of the love of music and dancing, we became better acquainted. After we found out they lived in the southern part of the state, just like us, we discovered we had a lot in common. Living in such tight quarters we soon became friends.

Unless you have lived through integration, it would be hard for you to understand how unusual it was to be such opposites in color and background. I was fortunate that I had experienced playing with negro children as a child so they were not as foreign to me, as they were to Arlene. In addition to music and dancing, we had one more had common interest. Each other's hair! Arlene had Indian blood so her hair was a beautiful black color and extremely coarse. My hair was thick and blond. The other two girls had black kinky curls. Their hair looked cute after they washed it, but they were not happy with the tight curls. They wanted their hair to be straight, and Arlene and I wanted ours to have large curls. We used large tin juice cans to wrap our hair around to create them. This was called a "bubble curl." My "bubbles" would last for a few days, but Arlene's would become straight overnight.

Sasha and Mabry liked to use a heavy metal comb which they heated over an alcohol burner to straighten their hair. They would take a bath in the tub and wash their hair. Then they would comb all the curls out to get rid of the tangles. Next, they would grease their hair with petroleum jelly, then pull the hot comb through a few thick strands. This would straighten it out so that they might style it. It always looked clean and shiny because of the color as well as the jelly. The bad part is the bathtub suffered with a greasy ring that black curly hair was stuck in, after they bathed and washed out the grease from the last style. Then the two of them would get in a fight over who had to clean the bathtub. I never understood this. Why didn't each of them just clean up after themselves? I think they enjoyed the "fight". Arlene and I didn't care as long as it was clean when we used the tub. With all of us having our own bedroom we were responsible for cleaning it and changing the linens. The hospital wanted the rooms to be neat and clean, so they would do a surprise inspection from time to time. I had mastered throwing my mess into some secret spot when I was home. I had attempted to do the same thing here. Mostly, I had adequate time before they came up to inspect. Arlene had learned my method so we rarely got caught. Mabry and Sasha were not so lucky. They took a scolding, time after time, but didn't improve at all until the inspector told them they were going to miss the movie this month if it happened again. They became neater than we were.

CHAPTER 30

HURTFUL HOME VISIT

My first time home on a pass was granted the week of New Year's Eve. There was a big party in my home town and most of my friends were home from college. An old boyfriend from grade school called and invited me to the party. I had a black dress that had been bought for a party that I had not been able to attend before I went to the hospital. It was perfect to wear to the party, so I accepted. Now I needed to get my hair done before I attended, so I called the lady that had always done my hair. She was completely filled up, fixing everyone's hair for the New Year parties. She was so happy to hear from me that she said she would work me in some way if I would come late that day.

I did and when I walked into her shop, everyone in there was someone I knew. They all were happy to see me, except one girl who I had attended school with. Everyone was chattering about how glad they were I was able to come home for the holidays when this girl said, "I can't believe you want to be in the same room with her breathing all her germs. We're taking a chance on getting that horrible disease!" She turned to the beautician and said, "I'm not staying here, and you won't be getting any more of my business unless you ask her to leave!' The beautician said,

"This is my beauty shop, and I don't think it's appropriate for you to tell me who I can and cannot have for a customer. Is there anyone here that has a concern about Lydia staying?" No one responded. She looked around the room in disgust. The girl ripped off her cape, threw it in the floor, then grabbed her purse and coat. She threw open the door, walked out, turned to glare at me and slammed the door.

I was shocked! I was thinking, "I haven't been positive since the last of August and was only there waiting for the 6- month time limit to expire." My eyes welled up with tears! I thought is this going to be something I have to deal with for the rest of my life? My mind was full of lots of thoughts about how Daddy wasn't interested in being friends with people from our home-town. Was the real reason not the embarrassment about being an alcoholic for so long, but instead being shunned by people afraid of our disease. I looked at the group standing there, some in their makeup capes, hair rollers and some with their heads wrapped up in a towel and wondered if they were thinking the same thing about me. I decided to tell them about being negative, and how I didn't pose a threat to any of them. I hugged the beautician and apologized for running off her customer. Everyone was so sweet and gracious to me that I was grateful for this small town "faith-fulness" that had been displayed in this small beauty shop.

This incident had ruined my first free day at home, because now I worried about going to the party tonight and having others being afraid of me. The beautician said she was sorry that I had such an unfriendly welcome home. I waited to be worked in after the others and had a nice visit. I looked ready for a party after she had styled my hair. It looked so much better than what I had attempted to do to it the past 6 months. This was a boost to the "ego." I felt a lot better about myself.

When my date picked me up, I told him about what happened at the beauty shop and he said he was not concerned. He said, "It's all over town. You know how gossip travels in a small town." Then we entered the party, and I was very apprehensive that it might dampen the atmosphere of a good time, but I was wrong. We had a great time and none of my friends were afraid of being infected, and everyone was glad to see me.

After the short visit I was returned on the 2nd day of January to the Sanatorium. My last culture was to come back the last of January, so I was on "pins and needles" waiting for the outcome. Arlene was increasingly blue because hers was due shortly after mine.

The night before the results were given to me, I agonized over every little thing I might have done wrong. I was afraid I hadn't let myself gain enough weight to hold off another infection, I was afraid I had done too much physically to heal properly, afraid I had not rested enough during the day (I never napped but instead read books during rest time, morning and evening) and particularly afraid I hadn't prayed enough. It was too late now!

I woke up early to a miserable depressing winter day. Mid-morning they finally called me to the doctor's office. I sat down in the chair, thinking of the last time I was in this position praying that I would be going home. It never happened, and I didn't think I could bear it again. A few minutes later the doctor came in and sat down with his file. He said Lydia I have good news for you. Your final culture is back, and you have been negative, for 6 months, so you are eligible to go home. The bad news is you cannot go to college until this coming fall as we want you to be totally well. You have to have 8 hours sleep a night and right now if I let you go, you would probably be involved in college life, and not get that required sleep. You will continue to take the 27 pills a day for 2 more years. You will have a chest X-ray every year for the next several years and if you are smart, you will take good care of yourself from now on. This disease is not gone from your body, it is in remission, and will stay so if you take the precautions to keep it that way. Otherwise, we will be seeing you back here in the future. You have had it twice so you should understand what I am talking about. You may call your parents and have them come get you tomorrow. All your paper-work will be ready when they arrive.

I told Arlene, and I could see her fighting back the tears. I said, "You will be out of here in a few weeks. Think how happy your family will be to see you." She didn't say a word. We were going to be parting the same way we had met as she started edging back into the "introvert" I had met when she arrived.

CHAPTER 31

GOING HOME

The next day, my parents arrived at noon. I sought out Arlene and hugged her. I told her I would pray for her negative report. We parted without another word from her. My parents went into town for lunch then we started the long ride home.

The first few days, I did nothing but sleep late and put things away. I kept thinking "What am I going to do until fall?" My parents wanted to treat me like an invalid and see to it that I repeated the same protocol that the hospital had for me. I was so bored. My old boyfriend that had gone with me when I checked into the hospital, reappeared and we started dating. He was a year younger than me and a Senior in high school. He would come to see me every night for a short period of time, as I was still having to keep the tight schedule for rest. Once school was out, we were together constantly and a romance developed that we probably were both too young to have.

My parents didn't want me involved with him because they thought it might keep me from going to college in the fall. They asked me to break up with him and see some other boys. They should have used some reverse psychology, because this only drove us closer together. Before the summer was over, he said,

"Why don't we get married? I can talk to my sister in California and see if I might get a job with her husband in construction. It really pays good and I could get my GED at night?" I don't know what we were thinking, but we ran off and married in another state that only required you to be 18. I went back home and tried to keep the secret until we could figure out how to get to California.

There was no way to keep this secret and when my parents found out they were furious. They called me into the living room and told me that they were going to get an annulment. I told them I didn't want an annulment and was old enough to get married whenever I wanted. The argument became so bad, that Daddy took his belt out of his trousers and said, "I have never whipped you in your life, but I am going to beat some sense into you tonight!" I turned quickly and ran out the door. I could hear them arguing about who was going after me which gave me the opportunity to get a head start. It was late, and I had no place to go. I knew that they would be looking for me at his house. The key to the car was in my bedside table, so I decided to walk to Edith's. I took all the back alleys until I reached her home. It was summer, so I went to her bedroom window and whispered through the screen "Edith, wake up!" I had to repeat this twice before she heard me and let me in. I got in her bed and told her what had happened, and that I was hiding from my parents. I did not tell her that I was married. At that moment, the phone in their house rang and I knew it was my parents calling! I heard her mother say, "Hello" into the phone and then "No, I have not seen her." Then she said, "I will ask Edith if she knows where she might be." She laid the phone down on the table and started down the hall. I slid out of the bed and laid between the bed and the wall as her mom walked in. She said, "Edith, wake up, the Constantines are calling and Lydia has run away. Have you seen her or do you know where she might be? Edith acted as though she had just been awakened and said, "No, I do not." Her mother went back to the phone and told my mother about the conversation with Edith and she hoped they found me.

I left before daylight and waited in the barn. They finally left for work, so I went in the house and called Steven and told him Daddy might be looking for him. He told me his father had already confronted Daddy, and that he had all his belongings together. He told me his father had a suggestion for us.

The car was still in the garage and mother had not found my key. I suppose she thought I had it with me. I packed up to move to California. I drove to his house and we put everything we had in my convertible. His father had given him some money. I had a lot of savings bonds from the money that my Uncle Billy had given me through the years to help with college. We used that money to make our trip. My parents were searching all over for us that morning. The moment everything was packed, we gassed up and left. We were headed to Ontario, CA because his sister and brother-in-law lived there. He could get a job in construction where the brother-in-law worked. They gave him the job the first day. This had been his father's suggestion. His father was afraid my Daddy might hurt Steven, so this would be a good distance to be away, until everything cooled down.

What we didn't know is that someone saw my car leaving town and called my parents. They then called the state patrol, told them I had stolen the car, and they were not sure where we were going, but they wanted us arrested. They did not find us in time, so we went over the state line where the patrol had no jurisdiction headed west.

CHAPTER 32

CALIFORNIA 1962

Once we arrived, we stayed with his sister's family until we found a duplex we could afford. It was new and furnished, but it backed up to the desert, and they had put up a tight picket fence to keep the sand from blowing against the house. There were grapevines on the fence, so we watered them and had grapes during the season. There was no yard. It was a concrete pad painted green. It was a one bedroom but it was roomy.

I had to find a place to work also. I applied at a Newberry Company and took a job using a "computer." It was a huge machine that sat in the floor, and all the items the company sold had "punch cards" attached to the item for sale, or in the box with them. My job was to take the cards when the item was sold and when I had collected enough for the day, I would put them through this computer. This process showed what had been sold, when it had been sold and how much inventory was left. I'm sure it told other things also, but I have forgotten. I had seen the job listed in the newspaper and applied. I had to take a test to see if I might be qualified to learn this, and I passed.

Since I had never lived in a large city, it did not occur to me that I should have asked where the job was located. It was twenty miles through heavy traffic on a freeway. I had never driven on anything but a two- lane road. The first day I went to work, the traffic was driving so fast and the horns honking, and I was on the access road, driving on the ramp, preparing to enter at the next access. When I saw what I was driving into I prayed, because I thought this was my last day. Horns blared at me and some guy rolled his window down to tell me I was in the wrong lane. He was right! I could not figure out how to read the signs, and I missed my turn. Finally, 5 minutes before the time I was to clock in, I was there.

Everyone was very nice, except the man they called the floor manager. He was not patient with someone who was new at this job. He finally took me to a lady in the back of his floor and told her to show me what to do. She was very kind and by the end of the day, I had learned most of the job.

Steven and I were running out of money, and the first pay day was not for another week. When we had first arrived, there were other people from our part of the country living there, and his sister had a wedding shower for us. We had received some nice gifts, but had not used them yet. We didn't have enough money for groceries. We did not want to borrow from his relatives, so we took back some of the shower gifts and used the money to buy groceries. At that time there was no such thing as a credit card.

We did not have any other money to spend, except for $20.00 in a checking account, that we had opened with the savings bond money we had left from the trip out there. I took the money from the gift sale to the grocery store and I had a list. Each time I bought something on the list I put the price by it. When I got to the check- out I added up the items and found I didn't have enough money, so I picked out things I didn't absolutely need, and put them back. I had a $1.23 when I left the store. On the way home, I remembered that Sunkist had piles of their citrus fruit that anyone could pick through discarded by their plant. The fruit was good, but not perfect enough to go to market. We drove by there and picked through the oranges, lemons, grapefruits and limes. We both took our lunch every day that week and drank water until we got our paychecks. Once again, I was getting a character builder and so was he.

California was fun in the early 1960s, the hippies were just beginning to show up, you could get to the beach easily and surfing was the "bomb." The weather was perfect and the music coming out of the radio was several months ahead of what was being played back home.

A young couple moved into the duplex next to us. We were excited as we thought we could befriend them and know someone besides just family. When they moved in, we introduced ourselves and volunteered to help them move some of their items in the house. They said they needed no help and did not appear to want to befriend us. This was a beginning of a strange situation.

After they were there for about a week and seemed to be settled in, they left the house and did not return until the following week-end. They had a baby bed and baby equipment that they were moving in the house. We assumed that they were pregnant and were getting ready for the baby. I never got a chance to congratulate them, as every time I would step out of the house, they would immediately go back inside. My husband said I was trying too hard and if they didn't want to be friends I should leave them alone.

The following week, we were in the family room which backed up to their bedroom, and we could hear a baby crying. We could also hear them yelling at each other. What they were saying was not very clear, but I did hear something that he said about quieting the baby. The next night at about the same time, our house was dark as they we were trying to watch tv and leave all the other lights off in order to save money on the electricity. We heard a car pull up between our drives and two doors closed.

A young man said, "Let me take care of this, as I'm not sure about this couple." We started watching through the shades and turned off the TV. Apparently, our neighbors were watching for them to pull up, as they opened the door before they knocked. They went inside and stayed for quite a while. The two men raised their voices, but we could only make out one part of the conversation. It involved how healthy the child was and where did he come from. One said, "I want to have him examined." The other said, "No, not without a deposit!" Had we been able to afford a newspaper, we would have known that someone had been taking babies out of the city, some were Hispanic and some from local unwed Caucasian mothers to sell to parents that were wanting to adopt. These parents said they had been put on a long waiting list and anxious to get a child. They said they had decided that it would be better buying from these baby markets, instead of waiting years to go through the normal channels for adoption.

After more negotiating outside, the baby left with the couple in the car. We were astounded! We were not sure what it was we had just viewed. We were young and pretty naïve. The traffic next door began to get busier. One day at work, my husband heard some people discussing "baby trafficking." He stopped to listen and didn't say a word. When he came home that night, he told me that there was going to be something on the TV that night that had already appeared in the newspaper.

The news story was about a young girl who had been contacted by a couple, because she was pregnant and unmarried. They asked if she would be interested in finding a home for her baby when it was born. She told them she didn't know what she was going to do, but she had not thought of adoption. They told her they had personal contacts who were willing to see that her baby reached a good home, and that they were willing to pay her for this transaction. The amount was a $1000. She gave them her information then told them she would call after the baby was born. They gave her a card that indicated they were in the adoption business. When the time came, she was to give up the baby and receive the money. When they came by to pick up the infant, they gave her an envelope full of cash, bundled up the baby and left.

The next day, she had misgivings. At first, she was too embarrassed to call the police and ashamed she had sold her child. With much encouragement from her family, she finally went to the police. Once she had revealed this to the police, several other young women came forward with the exact same problem.

It was only 4 days later, when we were awakened in the middle of the night by flashing lights and a policeman with a bullhorn, demanding the people next door come out with their hands up. Our neighbors next door and the couple that visited them weekly, were arrested. The police knocked on our door to ask us, if we had anything to tell them about the people next door. We truly didn't and so were never questioned again. But this is what we found out about them later.

The first couple who came to visit in the car were getting babies in a scheme called "gray market baby" adoptions. They would pay young unwed mothers for their baby and take it straight from the hospital in California, acting as though they were family members and using falsified birth certificates. They would leave them with our next- door neighbors, who would then pack up the baby and take it to Nevada to someone willing to pay large sums of cash for this child. The neighbors soon discovered they could make more money finding their own mothers and selling cheaper, directly to the purchasing parents.

According to the TV, sometimes, the pregnant woman would be kept in housing by a lawyer until they delivered instead of being in the hospital. At this time in history, it was not illegal to alter birth records in the case of adoption. Supposedly, this was to protect the birth mother from being contacted by the adoptee later. This was the lawyer's job. Our neighbors were apparently easier to catch than the "gray market baby schemers." This arrest gave a lot of attention to the baby trafficking and just about closed all of this shameful bunch down in the state of California and Nevada.

About the same time, I had my own pregnancy to contend with. We had not spoken to my parents since we had come to California. They had found out where we had gone and got our telephone number from my husband's family, who were still speaking to us. When they called, they said they knew a baby was on the way, and they wanted me to come home. Someone had told me that my father was so miserable about my leaving home that he had lost over 15 pounds. We told them we could not return home because we both had a job and if we came home, there was no job or source of income. They told us that my husband's father was going to hire him to work at the Grain Company that he managed. My parents did not want me to work because of my condition. I was still taking 27 pills a day to control my tuberculosis, and pregnancy caused hormonal problems that might make me lose my negative condition. No one ever worried about the medications and how it would affect the baby during the 60's. My large dosage should have hurt my child, but the Lord wanted him to be healthy and so he was.

We said "No." A couple of weeks later, I was beginning to "show." It was not very obvious but within a few more weeks, I was called into the office at work. The Floor Manager asked me outright "Are you pregnant?" I said, "Yes, why?" He said, "It is the company's policy not to hire pregnant women. Your job is finished here. Get your things together and I will get your final check." I was so stunned! I felt the heat rising in my cheeks. I didn't want to go home. I wanted to be independent.

When I arrived home, my husband said, "We'll have to go home. My Dad made me an offer to work with him. The money I will be paid at home, will be adequate as it will be almost as much as the two of us are making right now." Reluctantly, and with a knot in my throat, I called my parents. They said they wanted to send money to make sure we had enough for gas and food on the way home. We packed up all our things that weekend and left for home. I was to drive when we started until I got tired, and then he would drive until we couldn't stay awake.

We left early and had made it 79 miles to Barstow, CA. It was a much higher elevation than the area we had lived in. On the way down the mountain, I had to use the brake a lot, because it was such a steep decline for someone so inexperienced. I did not know to put it in a lower gear. All of a sudden, when I hit the brake, it would not slow the car down! My husband yelled, "Slow down!" I screamed, "I have no brakes!" There were many curves, so the car kept getting faster and faster I was moving up toward 100 miles an hour and it was all I could do to keep it on the road, as we came upon curve after curve. I was praying that nothing would be in front of me, as there was a lot of oncoming traffic. Just as I reached a spot where it was beginning to level off, I came upon a small car that was moving very slowly and pulled out quickly to pass him. Coming up the incline was a large truck which left me no place to go! My heart was in my mouth and I knew we were going to be killed! I ran the big truck and the little car off the road! I went right between the two vehicles. I couldn't believe it!

The high speed continued but we managed to get to the bottom of the grade. The car finally began slowing down. We had hit the level terrain coming into a small town. I still was speeding and was looking for the first opportunity to get off the road and let it roll to a stop. I passed a police man, sitting on the side of the road in a patrol car. He saw me speeding and turned his siren on and started following us. There was a curve coming up in front of me, where I saw a pile of gravel on someone's business yard. I pulled off the road and headed toward the gravel. When I hit it, the impact was more than I anticipated, but it did bring us to a stop. What a relief from the agony of the ride down. I couldn't move and shut off the motor and just sat there.

Immediately, the police were on us. They jumped out of the car, and one pulled out his pistol and ordered us out of the car. We got out, and he stared chastising me about trying to kill people, not obeying the law, etc. I was so shaken that all I could do was stand there quietly and take it while tears were welling up in my eyes. I was so grateful to be alive that I fell to my knees and bent over and sobbed. Between sobs, I said, "We have no brakes." The policeman turned to his partner and said, "Get a mechanic". He did and the mechanic verified that I was right. The police became a lot nicer, especially after they noticed I was pregnant. They took us to a local motel for the night. They hauled the car off to be repaired. I called my parents, and they sent the money to pay for the repair on the car. The next afternoon we started out again and had nothing else eventful happen on our return.

CHAPTER 33

BACK WHERE WE STARTED

When we reached his parent's house it was late evening, and they met us at the door. They had prepared for us to stay that evening. We called my parents and told them where we were, and that we would be at their house the next morning. We went to bed early and were exhausted after the lengthy trip. I dreaded seeing my parents after running away. When we arrived, both of them seemed excited to see us. One glance at Daddy confirmed what I had heard about the weight loss. He looked almost as thin as when he had tuberculosis. My mind was racing, I was asking myself, "Is he sick again or has he started drinking again?" I felt guilty because I had been told that he was miserable that I had left. I walked up to him and hugged him and surprisingly, he hugged me back. He smiled, and I thought, "He has missed me."

Mother was unusually chatty. She was wanting to know all the particulars about my health and the baby. In a few seconds of her conversation, I knew why. She said "Maybe this will be a boy." I said, "Or maybe it will be a girl." Her expression changed, so I started talking about finding someplace to rent. Mother said, that "Big Momma," (my grandmother that went to California every winter) was leaving in about a week for her winter trip. She wanted us to use her house which was in a neighboring town, and she did not want any money for it. She just wanted us to pay the utilities and any other small expenses. I was relieved that we would not be in the same town as our parents, as I could feel all our independence evaporating. My husband said, "That will be fine." He didn't even ask me what I wanted to do. But with no other options, I guess I would have had to comply anyway.

We moved in that day. We had a very small amount of belongings. "Big Momma" was still there. It was very comfortable house, except that the family room and kitchen were the only rooms heated and air conditioned, but the bedrooms and bathroom were not. When the door was closed to the bedrooms, there was neither heating or cooling. Big Momma gave us a featherbed to put on the bed and a feather comforter to put over us. Feathers are much heavier than down. Once you got into the bed and pulled the comforter over you, it was very difficult to change your position or roll over.

My husband started the job his father had given him. This required a thirty-five mile drive to work located in another state, 5 days a week, in our only car. After Big Momma left for California, this meant I had no transportation, so I was limited to where I could go. I had walked downtown to a store that carried books because I wanted to find out how to be a mother. My knowledge was so limited. I had never played with dolls as a child and had only held my best friend, Edith's nephew once when he was first born. I had never changed a diaper, fixed a bottle or knew anything about nurturing. I could not find the book I wanted, but after I found a local obstetrician, he told me of a pharmacy that had a book by Doctor Spock for any questions a new mother might have. The pharmacy was in the same building as his office, so I purchased a thick paperback called, "Baby and Childcare." This book for me was the "Bible" of child raising. I took it home and read it from cover to cover, then I read it again and marked all the pertinent passages that I thought

I needed the most. In my mind, I became an authority on childcare.

My husband became a different person when he got back to his friends. They were all young single guys and running around at night drinking and chasing women. He would take our car and leave me at the house at night. This became a regular pattern, and he began to drink a lot even though he was under age. When he would come home, he would become mean and spiteful. He was not the same person I had married, and this drinking problem reminded me of my dad. In all of Daddy's drinking years, he had never struck my mother. I was not so lucky. He slapped me when he came in one evening because I had asked him where he had been. This started a repetitive abusive habit.

On the night before Thanksgiving, we were preparing to go to his parents the next day. Once again, he left to go see the boys. When he got back it was after 11 o'clock, and I had fallen asleep. The door was locked and he was pounding on the door and yelling obscenities at me. When I opened the door, he grabbed me by the arms and pushed me down and kicked me in the leg. Then he yanked me up by my hair and hit me in the eye with his fist. I was still sleepy and half wondered if this was a bad night-mare. I fell down trying to protect my stomach, because I was fearful he would kick me again, and injure the baby. All of a sudden, he stopped and walked off to the bathroom. I could hear him throwing up.

I took this opportunity to grab my coat, shoes and purse and run out the door! He had the keys to the car so I was on foot. I ran down the side of the house to the next street which was not well lit. I thought it would be easier to hide on that street. I heard our car start up and, I slipped against the wall of a house as he went by. After that I continued down the next street with no idea of where I was going. All of a sudden, I heard a car coming and realized it was him. He had turned off his lights and had spotted me when I came out of the shadows. He pulled up beside and was crying. He said, "I am so sorry, please get in the car and come home, I'll never do that again." I said, "I am afraid to get in the car. You are not the man I married." He said, "Get in please, I promise I won't hurt you." I got in and he was fine the rest of the night. We slept late and had to hurry to get ready to go to his parent's house. I looked in the mirror and I had a black eye and a bruise on the other side of my face. I had a horrible bruise on my leg which I could cover up, but there was no way to cover my face. I expected him to say we are not going, but instead he said, "We'll tell them you fell." I looked at him and said, "Okay."

When we arrived at his house and opened the front door, his family and 5 siblings were already there. The conversation stopped when they saw me. We told them the story that we had rehearsed. I saw his father's face get red, and he asked him to come in the other room. Their conversation became so heated that everyone could hear it. His Father said, "You both are lying to me! She didn't fall! You have hit her! If you ever touch her again, I will beat you half to death!" (This was no idle threat as his father had been a "Golden Glove" participant during the war). Next his father said, "You are lucky if her father doesn't kill you first. What has come over you? You need to quit running with that trashy group of boys, who are single, plus you definitely need to stay away from alcohol, as it makes you mean." Steven said in a very meek voice, "I promise I won't do it again." This put a damper on the holiday. His family were such good people that I couldn't imagine what they were thinking. Everyone was struggling to act festive when no one felt it.

I dreaded for my parents to see me as they were coming over the next day. When the morning came and my parents arrived, I discovered his father had already talked to my dad, and they were not cordial to my husband. Mother had brought lunch, and we sat down to eat and the conversation was about getting prepared for the baby.

The next day my mother called and asked if he was there. I said, "No." and she said in a hateful voice, "I want to tell you that you will have to learn how to control this problem. You've made your bed and you'll have to lay in it. I stayed with your father through all the bad things that he did and you will have to, also. You can't leave the father of your child. No one in our family has ever had a divorce, and you will just have to learn how to cope with the problem if it happens again. I suspect you may be doing something to provoke it. You have no source of support since you have no job, and don't ask to come back home." I was shocked and said, "Don't worry, coming back home would be my last choice." And I hung up the phone. Had she forgotten that Daddy was never a mean drunk and had never hit her?

About a week later, on a Saturday afternoon, we were watching tv. Mother and Daddy knocked on the door. When we opened it, they stopped in the doorway. They told the two of us to get in the car. They said they had a surprise for us. We complied and they took us back to my hometown where they drove into a new sub-division of nice homes, across the county road from our farm. They stopped in front of a new brick and limestone ranch style house. They said, "This is your new home. We just bought it for you." I was sick to my stomach. They wanted to be the control-ling element of my life.

I could see Daddy doing this, but was shocked to see Mother allowing it. After Daddy had seen my black eye, I thought, "He is trying to get me close enough that I can come to him if I have to." After my recent conversation with Mother, I didn't want the house and didn't know how to tell them. My husband seemed really pleased to have it and told them how much he appreciated it. They said to get out of the car and we'd go look at the inside. It had a beautiful limestone fireplace that took up one whole wall, draperies and lots of built ins. It was a new house, professionally decorated. I told them it was very nice, but we'd like to talk about it and Steven said, "I'm all for it, what do you want to talk about Lydia?" I said "I'm not sure we have the income to support this house." Daddy said, "We'll see how that goes, if you need help, we'll help you." I could see I was not on the winning side. So now we have a house to live in. They handed the keys to Steven and said, "We have another set in case you lock yourself out." (My advice is never let your parents have a key to your house and always ask them to knock before they come in. Better yet, never let them buy you a house.) We moved in the next week, and I began to put a nursery together for the baby.

It was getting closer to what we thought was my delivery date, and I received a letter from the Sanatorium telling me I was due back for a chest X-ray and exam, as I was still on the medication. The appointments were set for the following week. The Sanatorium did not want me to make a 5 hour trip any closer to my due date. Mother, Steven and I made the trip over in one day. After spending the night, my tests were scheduled for early morning so that we might go home the same day. That night I laid in bed and agonized about the tests, and what I would do if I were "positive." I had seen 2 girls who were there when I was in the hospital who were positive. When their baby arrived, it was taken away from them to avoid exposure for the child. I did not want that to happen to me or my baby. I had no delusions that lead me to believe this could not happen to me, since I had not finished my medication schedule as I should have before getting pregnant. I had another year of 27 pills a day to go.

I dreaded seeing my doctor who would read the X-rays and all the other tests to me. I was doing some heavy praying for a good result and wishing I had my friend's Rosary for added support. I recited what I remembered from the many nights she and I prayed it together. I wanted all my bases covered! This was no longer a prayer request for me. This was for this little unknown child I was carrying, and who I had vowed to love and take care of for his/her lifetime. My intention was to make sure that I did not remain distant as Mother had with me. I also pledged that I would never let anything or anybody endanger his/her life including myself with my health problems.

We arrived at the Sanatorium mid-day, and they were ready for me. I completed all the tests and went to my doctor's office to wait. My nerves were shot! I couldn't carry on a conversation with anyone. All my thoughts were swirling around in my brain and nothing was coming to surface that I could talk to anyone about sensibly. The doctor came in and sat down. He gave me a good report! He said I should come back after the birth and be checked again. He cautioned me about doing too much activity and traveling long distances! (Too late for that) I was so relieved to have the good news, I could have jumped across the desk and hugged his neck. The ride home was a lot more pleasant.

The next day I got up and began to have what I thought might be labor pains. This was too early for what we thought was the delivery date, so I told my mother and she called the doctor. As a precautionary measure, he had me come to his office to be checked. He was shocked that I had ridden 11 hours in a car in two days. He said this was probably causing the pains and advised us to check into the hospital to make sure I was not going into premature labor. Since I had these other health problems and was still taking all this medication, I was relieved he was putting me in there. After being in the hospital bed for about 9 hours, he said I appeared to be dilating. He said the baby was probably a little small for delivery and he had hoped we would be able to stall his progress.

Now it was obvious that the trip had been too much, and the baby was coming. This was the 12th of February and I laid there until the early morning hours of the 13th without food and little water hoping to deliver. I was having to take the 27 pills a day on an empty stomach and I was beginning to be nauseated. Soon, I was throwing up the pills and water and was unable to keep anything down. I was so miserable I did not think I could make it another day. Early morning on the 14th I delivered a 6lb, 1 ounce boy. I took one look at him with black hair and dark brown eyes and just like every first- time mother, it was "love at first sight." This was something that Dr. Spock did not cover in his book!

The baby could only get down 2 ounces of formula at a time as he would keep falling asleep. I could not breast feed him because of the high level of medication in my body. He was so tiny and within the next day he would begin to weigh less. He was in the 5 to 5 ½ lb range, and I was struggling to get enough formula down him to keep his weight up. The next day I was allowed to leave the hospital, but he had to stay until they could improve his weight. I did not want to leave him, so I came and stayed during the days. Once he could reach 6 pounds, I could take him home.

My husband, his parents, and my parents came to visit and spent most of their time looking through the viewing window. My mother and father were so excited you would have thought it was their child. I was the only one allowed to hold him and they both wanted me to bring him to their house as soon as he was released. The day I left for home with Seth (he was named after mother's brother). We went straight to mother's house where she met me at the door, took the baby into her arms and sat down in the rocker. I had brought him home in a blue gown that I had made for him, that was too large because he was so tiny. He was beginning to look pink and healthy, and his little face had lost the wrinkles he had when he was born.

As she rocked, Mother said "Why don't you leave him here, so you can go home and rest for a day or two. Then, I will come show you how to take care of him." I said, "No, thank you. I have been looking forward to his coming home and I have read the book, so I know what to do to take care of him." If I need your help I will call you. I can take care of him by myself." I stayed for a while and Daddy held him and they both seemed mesmerized by this baby. After about an hour, I told them I had to be home because my husband's family was coming to see the baby. I bundled Seth up and left.

On the way to the house my thoughts were melancholy. I knew that this was the boy they had always dreamed of having. Perhaps this would make their relationship with me better, since they finally could experience raising a boy like they had always dreamed. This could be a good thing.

I was worn out from the bottle feeding every 2 hours, and Seth would keep falling asleep. I would have to tickle his feet to wake him and help him to remember to nurse. This went on 24 hours a day, and I was really worn out by the 3rd day. I called Mother, as badly as I hated to, and asked her to take care of him for the day so that I might rest a while. That evening when I took him home, I was much more rested.

In 1963, a new baby was a job. You had to boil your bottles and nipples. Once the formula had been poured into the bottle, you put it in a pan of water and turned on the stove to warm it. The baby was usually crying at the top of his lungs waiting for the long process to take place so he might nurse. Pampers had just been invented and wouldn't you know my baby would be allergic to the perfume in them. That meant you had to use cloth diapers which were about 24" square. You would fold the squares into a diaper then use two safety pins to hold the sides together. On top of that you would use a rubbery panty to keep the diaper from leaking. If the baby had a bowel movement, you would undo the diaper and rinse the fecal matter out in the toilet then flush.

(One father, who was a friend of ours was babysitting for the first time. When he changed the diaper and saw the bowel movement, he decided he should first rinse the baby's butt by dipping the child in the toilet and rinsing it off. Next, he would rinse off the diaper. He told this story to his friends later and commented that the baby let out a "yelp" when his little bottom hit the cold water. They all laughed. His wife heard this story, but was not amused. He never baby-sat again.)

After rinsing the diaper then you would place it in a covered bucket called a diaper pail, full of water, soap and bleach or Borax. When the bucket got full, you would wring the diapers out by hand and wash them in a washing machine, if you had one, or in a tub. I had a washer, but no dryer so my dad put up a clothesline for me to hang them on. In the winter, when my baby was born, you had to pen the diapers on the line to dry. This resulted in a freeze-dried diaper, 24 inches square. At the end of the day, you took them down and they would be "stiff as a board." You then held them by the corners, took them in the house then laid them all around on the furniture until they thawed and were limp enough to fold.

There were no baby monitors or baby seats in cars. You could buy a seat with a little buckled strap that hung on the bench seat so that your baby could sit upright and see out. Some even came with a steering wheel so that the baby might drive. My best description of this "gadget" was it looked like a mechanism made to propel a baby through the windshield and onto the pavement out front. I was much more careful with my child. I selected to stand my child upright, and when an emergency came, I like millions of new mothers would throw my right arm out to hold him against the seat until the "danger" was over. This only failed one time when he was about three. He was standing upright in the passenger seat leaning on the back portion. Someone, pulled out in front of me, I hit the brake, and my quick response was a few seconds too long. The back of my right hand couldn't restrain him as he was already falling forward, and I caught him by the leg. He rolled into the floor and sat upright, luckily unharmed.

He said, "You did that on purpose and I am mad at you." Then he began to cry. I pulled over and picked him up to console him, so soon he was laughing and had forgiven me. It has never taken me long to understand where a problem is and to try to correct it. I decided from that day forward he could sit in his Pumpkin seat in the back and since he was strapped in, if I stopped too suddenly the seat might just slide off. I didn't think it would fall forward. It worked pretty good and was definitely safer than the front seat.

The rest of the year was pretty uninteresting. My husband worked and I stayed home with the baby. Steven began a pattern of infidelity that I did not know about during this time frame. He had reconnected again with some of his old single buddies and another one who was about to get married. He began going out on the week-end nights with this group and leaving me at home. He started drinking again. My parents were furious with him, as he was not being at all kind to them. One of the reasons he did not like them, is they used their key to come into our house, whenever they pleased. They never knocked or warned us they were coming, so sometimes we were not ready for company.

On November 23rd, 1963, Seth finally cut his first tooth when he was nine months old. That occasion stood out for me because he was just miserable with a swollen gum. I was sitting in the family room trying to rock him to sleep. At the same time, I was watching a soap opera named "As the World Turns" when Walter Cronkite interrupted a very emotional part of the show to tell the world that John F. Kennedy had been assassinated. I hung on every word about the President being taken to the hospital to find out how he was. At 1:30pm Walter Cronkite announced that he had died and began to weep. The whole country wept with him including me. In a very short time, all of the TV service went dead, and then for 4 days there was no programming. They would break in occasionally to alert the public about what was happening. The swearing in of Lyndon Johnson, and the arrest of the assassin were two of the "breaks." Once Lee Harvey Oswald, who had killed the President, was assassinated by Jack Ruby, the tv programming came back on. Everyone followed the saga until the time of Kennedy's burial. There was nothing else on tv. It was a very sad time in the United States.

CHAPTER 34

TRYING TO SALVAGE A MARRIAGE

My husband continued to get worse with his week-end parties while getting meaner at home. I tried to stay out of his way, but he began to try to brutalize me again. I told his father, and he said he was going to tell him to move out of the house, and instead go to a nearby town to live. He felt that our independence from my parents might bring us closer together. He was planning on enrolling him in college. He thought this would help get him away from the buddies, plus get him an education so that he might be able to get a good job. He said he would help us financially for the next 4 years, but I would have to get a job to pay our household expenses, and he would pay the rent and tuition. We agreed to do it.

We moved out of the house and into an apartment in the college town. Steven started his classes, and at night I would help him with his homework. He had a particularly hard time with bookkeeping so we worked on it every day. The town had a transit system so I rode it to look for work the first day and he took the car to school. I had seen a job opening at Finance and Commercial Lending Co. for a bookkeeper and applied for it first. When I went in and introduced myself, the interviewer took all my information, and then told me that the job had already been filled. I asked why they took my information and he said they were a national company that used a test to see if you were right for the job. The other person's test had come back that she was borderline. He said if his boss would allow it, they would give me the test and see what I made. Next, he asked me if I had bookkeeping experience and something made me say, "Yes." I thought I could finish studying my husband's class book and learn what I needed to know. I took the test, and the next morning they called to say I had a high score and to report to work Monday. I had only had 3 jobs in my life, a soda jerk in high school at a good friend's business that only lasted one day. I couldn't keep all the fountain products straight, so he told me that he didn't think that I was the right one for the job. The second job was working for a department store in town, making 50 cents an hour working on the week-ends plus wrapping gifts for Christmas. My third job was in California working in the new computer filing systems, where I was fired for being pregnant. When I got this job, it would be the 4th job that I applied for that I was hired for. I had never been turned down, but this could be the time. I spent the whole week-end studying book-keeping.

The one thing I could not do was get pregnant again because I would be in danger of the TB reoccurrence. Also, I would not be able to keep this job I had just started. I had found out employers never let you work while you were "showing." Birth control was new, and I had started taking pills right after my son's birth. This made my daily pill intake 28 pills a day instead of the 27, I had been taking for the TB control. The new pill was so potent that most women would be nauseous on and off all month, except for the days they were off of them, while having their periods. I would take the birth control at night so that if I did vomit in the morning, I would not be throwing up my other pills, as that would have done me no good. Closer to noon, I would take 9 of the 27 and work the others in before dinner. My dosage for the 27 pills didn't end until February 1, 1964.

I loved the job and it paid pretty good for the time. Before the end of the first semester of school my husband began to run with another group of guys, and I again was spending a lot of time alone with the baby. It was summer, and I had gotten a small blow-up pool for my toddler. I put it out in the backyard one beautiful summer day and put on a two- piece bathing suit. I went outside to sunbathe and let the baby enjoy the pool. I was facing to soak up the sun and felt like someone was watching me. I turned around and saw a man who was our next- door neighbor standing in the yard looking at me. He said, "I wanted you to know that you shouldn't wear skimpy suits like that, because that entices men to do bad things." I was shocked and said, "Men could not see me in my back yard, unless they came up as close to the house as you are." He said, "I'm a policeman and I'm just trying to keep you safe." "I said "Thank you." I picked up Seth and dried him off and went in the house. There was something about his demeanor that made me uncomfortable. I told my husband, and he said to keep the doors locked.

About a week later, I had dressed for bed in what they called, "Baby Doll pajamas." (They were sheer pajamas that were cut low at the neck and barely hung below the hips. Under them you wore matching panties.) We had no air conditioning, so the windows were open and the shades pulled up. The house set up high so the windows were high enough that no one could see in, unless you had a ladder. I went into the kitchen to fix a bottle for Seth, and thought I had seen something move outside the window. I didn't say a word and went into the living room to where my husband was sitting. I whispered to him about what I had seen, so he sneaked out the front door, around to the back of the house. To give him time to get there, I walked back and forth across the living room and kitchen, acting as though I was talking to my husband.

It turned out that the policeman was on the ladder peeping into our house. When my husband caught him, he apologized. My husband told him that he was going to report him to the police department if he didn't stay away from our house.

Shortly after that my husband got his grades, and I discovered that he had not been attending classes and had "flunked out." He had been leaving the house everyday supposedly to attend school, but instead he was riding around with his buddies. I had no idea what he did during the daytime as he was always home when I got there in the afternoon. I told his father and he told my parents. They asked us if we wanted to move back in the house, and my husband said, "Yes." He went back to work with his Father, and I gave up my job. I applied at a bank closer to home as it was too far for me to commute. The bank was building a new facility and would have a separate loan department. I took the job and worked at every level in the bank until the new bank was opened the following year. They paid me what I was receiving at the last job and had agreed to pay me more once the loan department was active.

The bad part is that I had a wonderful babysitter, when I was working before. Now my mother wanted to babysit every day while I worked. She pointed out how much money that would save me if she did it instead of hiring a babysitter. I finally agreed as there were few people willing to sit in this small town.

It was at this point of our marriage that it truly began to unravel. He was back on his routine with the guys and went out nearly every night. When he got his pay check, he quit paying the bills so that I was paying all of our expenses out of my earnings. He would cash his check and go out on Friday and spend the largest portion of it on the week end.

I then put him and our problems on the "back burner" because something was wrong with our son. He was swollen up in the groin area and cried if you touched that area while changing the diaper. I made an appointment and took him to the

CHAPTER 34

doctor. The diagnosis was a hernia, and they immediately put him in the hospital for surgery. While they were operating, they found another hernia on the other side and fixed it as well. When he came out of surgery, he was throwing up from the anesthesia which was ether at the time. He cried because he wanted me to be near him, so I climbed up into the large baby bed and held him, breathing the ether on his breath, until he fell asleep. Then I became nauseous from the ether.

When it was all over, we went home, and he required a lot of attention because he was in pain. My husband went out that night, and when he came back, I was still up with my child trying to help him calm down and go to sleep. My husband had been drinking and told me to make him shut up, as it hurt his head to listen to it. I picked him up and walked down the hall to the nursery. He followed me in and said, "Give him to me." I walked past him to the door and stopped in the kitchen. When I stopped, Seth started crying again. I set him down on the sofa, then started to sit beside him. At that point my husband slapped him and said, "Shut up!" and of course it made him cry harder. He slapped him again, and I ran into the kitchen and picked up a butcher knife! I would have killed him if he had touched him again! This was a side of me that I did not know existed! A sudden thought came to me that my child would have no parent if I did that. I laid the knife down while he was still hovering over him and said, 'If you want to hit somebody why don't you hit me, not a baby that's bandaged up from surgery and suffering already?" He turned and hit me in the stomach and kicked me with his cowboy boot two or three times. He told me that I was a "melodramatic bitch." I started fighting back which was a mistake and when it was over, he got in the car and left. I picked up the baby and put cold clothes on his cheeks to reduce the redness. I fixed him a bottle and fed him while I rocked him to sleep. My husband did not come back all night. The next day he called me again, told me how sorry he was, and how he was not going to do

197

it again. I was bruised and sore. The one thing he had learned after the intervention with his father, when I was pregnant is not to hit me where it shows.

One afternoon, a week later, I was coming in the backdoor and had picked up my son at Mother's and had an armload full of groceries. The phone rang, and I struggled to unload the groceries and put my toddler down. I ran to the phone and heard a strange man's voice on the other end. He said, "Lydia, I just thought you should know that your husband is having an affair and his girl- friend is pregnant." I had to look for a chair to sit down, I was so stricken by this information. I said, "Who are you, and who is the girl and where is she from?" He said, "This is Eddie Aarant. I'm not giving you her name but if you will go over to Sanford (a small town 15 miles from me) any evening, you will find the two of them at a local hangout. It's the only one in town so it won't be hard to locate. She told me that he told her he would marry her, if you would give him a divorce, but he says you won't do that. I just thought you ought to know and I wanted you to know that I have always wanted to date you. I wondered if you'd like to go out tonight and talk about this." I said, "I appreciate you calling me to tell me about this, but I have no interest in dating married men. Please do not call me again."

I got on the phone and called my friend, Marion who was another childhood friend. I asked her if she could pick me up after I fed my husband supper and take me someplace. She was very curious about what I had in mind. I told her I would call her as soon as he left, and I would explain when she got here. I hurried to fix supper and try to appear normal during dinner. I thought the time for him to leave would never come. But shortly after dinner, he said, "I'm going out" and walked out the door. I called Marion, and she picked my son and me up. I explained about the phone call and we headed to Sanford.

Marion said, "I've seen him with you at his most violent, when I tried to help pull him off of you. He hit me in the eye for trying to help. He gets meaner all the time and you would be better off without him." I was listening but not sure of how this was going to turn out.

Sanford is small, so it took very little time to find the hangout that he frequented. He was parked in the section that was a drive-in, and there happened to be a parking spot next to him on the driver's side. Marion pulled in. He had the window rolled down. They turned to look at us and when he saw me, I heard her say, "Who's that?" I said, "His wife and child, and he's lying to you about my not giving him a divorce." I said to Marion, "I'm through here. Let's go now." She backed out and we drove back home as fast as we could.

He must have dumped the girl out on the parking lot, because he was right behind us when we pulled into the garage. He jumped out of the car and came up and said, "I need to talk to you." I got out of the car and sat down in the garage on the back step and I said, "Marion, go get my Daddy if he hurts me or the baby." His face got so red, I thought he was going to explode! He said he could explain, and I listened the whole time he talked and thought how stupid does he think I am to believe all this garbage!

I knew the real reason he was trying to keep me from divorcing him. The Vietnam war was in full swing. If you were a single man and not in college, you were sure to be drafted. He was trying to avoid this and finally realized he could not treat me the way he had in the past and stay married. After an hour of talking and him apologizing again, I agreed to let him come in and spend the night. This was a Saturday, and on Monday I was going to find my way out of this mess. Regardless of Mother telling me I had no place to come if I left him, I was determined not to spend another week with him and endanger me and my son. For me when this came to an end, it was truly over.

CHAPTER 35

KNOWING THE END HAS COME

This was what I had in my mind. I knew like every woman that has been abused that there is no way the abuse will stop, unless you or he is dead. All the false promises are nothing but that. From what I had seen from other women who had experienced abuse, is that it will only accelerate as the years go by. He was not going to improve and now his abuse was trickling down to my child. I was afraid of him and knew I had to find my own way out. Mother had told me I was not welcome at home, but I really didn't want to go there anyway. If I had to, I would have asked Marion to let me move in until I found a place. I did not know how I was going to pay for it, but I knew the Lord would help me find a way.

When he left for work on Monday morning, I went to work and on my lunch hour, I went to see a lawyer who was a friend of our family. I told him I did not want my parents to know as they were against it. I also told him I wanted no child support or alimony as I had supported myself and us the whole time we had been married. The lawyer told me to go home, change the locks on the door, then go elsewhere to stay until he had time to cool down. They would serve him the next day with the divorce decree.

My husband was calling me when I reached home to tell me he was in Memphis picking up a partner of the company he worked for. He said he probably wouldn't be home until 10 o'clock. I said fine and we hung up. I had called a locksmith before I had left work to meet me to change the locks. I went in the house, took every piece of clothing in addition to anything else that belonged to him and put it in large boxes. I had not picked up Seth yet. Then I packed my clothing and my son's things and went to my parent's house.

When I walked in the house with Seth's belongings and my things, both my parents were shocked. Seth came running to me as he was always glad to see me. I picked him up and hugged him. Before I could say a word, my mother's first reaction was to reiterate what she had told me in the past. That I could not stay there and had to stay in the marriage because of my child. At that point I said, "I will not continue to be abused by him and especially now when he is starting to abuse Seth. I went to a lawyer today and filed for a divorce. They are going to serve him with the papers tomorrow. I am afraid of him and what he might do when he receives them. I'm only asking to stay here tonight so the two of us may feel safe. I'm not asking you to support us."

She started to speak again, when Daddy said, "You can stay as long as you want. You can live in this house the rest of your life if you want. I don't want you to be in danger and I certainly would be the first to protect you and Seth." Mother made her usual response by just walking out of the room. I'm sure Steven came looking for me and saw my car at my parent's house. I knew he would not come there as he was afraid of my dad. He did not attempt to break in our house.

The next morning, I got dressed and went to work. A little after lunch, I received a call from him. He had received the divorce papers. He was irate and threatening! He told me I could not have a divorce, and if I attempted to go through with it, he would see to it that I would lose my son. He said he had a friend who was willing to go to court and testify that he was having an affair with me. He said he would tell the court that I was nothing but a slut and an unfit mother. I had never been unfaithful and could not think of who he could get to perjure himself in court.

Later that week, a friend of mine called and told me that the perjurer was a good friend of my husband. I was shocked as I knew this man, as I had grown up with him and his brothers. I called the man's father and asked if I might visit with him. He said to come to his office, and we would talk. That afternoon when I left work, I went directly to his office. I sat down and told him the whole story. He said, "Don't worry about it. I guarantee you my son will not testify against you. I'm sure my son had good intentions. Most likely they were to keep your husband from being drafted. The Vietnam war is drafting mostly unmarried men and college drop outs. Since he has quit school plus getting a divorce he will probably come to the top of their list." I had not given the draft a thought but this item would not change my mind about the divorce. My thought was "He likes to fight. This will give him an opportunity to really fight for the good."

My husband sent his sister, Lora to see me. She was a friend and classmate of mine. She told me she had come to ask me not to divorce her brother. She said she knew he would be drafted and possibly sent to a war zone. She told me she was representing her whole family, and she was begging me not get the divorce. There was no turning back for me. I couldn't stand his infidelity after living all those years with Mother's unfaithfulness. The three things that I wanted in this marriage was a faithful husband, no alcoholism, and a man who loved my son as much as I did. Lora's family had been so good to me that it hurt me to tell her, "No," but I did. She cried, and I cried but there was no other way out of this dangerous situation. I did not want to be one of those women who allowed themselves to be abused. Whether the fear of leaving was a financial one, the embarrassment of breaking up the family, or the false belief that each time he hurt you and apologized that it would not happen again, divorce was the only answer to real peace and safety. I had to keep my focus on what was best for my son and me. I knew it would be difficult to support him by myself but I would starve before I remained with an abusive man. My husband started calling me to tell me how he could not live without me. In my heart I knew he really meant, "I have to have you to avoid the draft." These calls came at home and at work every day. They usually ended with a flare-up of his temper. He wanted me to meet him or let him come by to see me after work. I would not consent to that, and I knew he wouldn't come to my parent's house. I could tell Daddy was happy I was divorcing him, but Mother never mentioned it nor did I.

Because of what he was telling all over town about my "sins," I felt compelled to take a "character" witness to court with me. On October 1, 1965, I went to court to see the Judge who would determine what my future would be. Neither of my parents nor his came. What I was not expecting was the quiz that I received about my wifely duties. He asked me if I had cooked his meals, washed and ironed his clothes. I said, "Yes". Then he asked me if I had been a faithful wife. I said, "Yes." He then asked my husband if he had provided for me and my son and been a faithful husband and he said "Yes." "Then what is the reason for a divorce?" My lawyer said, "He has been physically abusive and unfaithful. Also, Lydia has worked to provide for her family and paid all the bills from her income." The judge asked him if he had proof of that and my lawyer said, "Yes". I was surprised that they didn't say anything to my husband about his infidelity lie.

At that point instead, they asked my character witness who was a deputy sheriff a few questions about my character and also about the abuse as well as the lack of support from my husband. The Deputy said that there was no reason to suspect infidelity on my part, then he added that I taught Sunday School at the local church, every Sunday and always brought my son with me. My lawyer told the court that I was not asking for child support or alimony. All I was asking for was custody of my son. After several other questions and answers the judge told us he was granting the divorce, and that I would receive custody of Seth. He would consider visitation rights monthly for my husband which he would reveal at a later date. This frightened me, as I was afraid, he might do something to Seth to spite me, if he had him alone. The judge also assigned me child support even though I had requested neither alimony nor child support.

I went home to move out of my parent's house and back into mine. My dad gave me two things, a loaded pistol and a yellow Ford Mustang Fastback. The car was for my transportation to my job 24 miles away as the car I presently had was experiencing a lot of repairs, due to high mileage. The gun was for protection alone at my house. He said, "I know you can shoot shotguns and rifles, but I would like to take you out and do some target practice with this pistol." We practiced until he thought I was proficient enough to handle it, then I took it home and put it under my pillow. I never did have to use it. I gave it back a month later. I also changed my telephone number. What I did not know is that my father was parking in our farm field, behind the fence line and trees, watching the house nightly. He was not clearly visible. The only thing dividing his farm field from my house was a county road that used to be a dirt road. He had a clear view of anyone pulling in my drive and attempting to pull in the front or the side door to the back entry. If my ex ever attempted to come by, I'm sure he would have detected it.

CHAPTER 36

BACK IN THE DATING POOL

The next week after my divorce, a male friend of mine asked me out. He was a jovial fun person to be around and he liked to do some of the same things I enjoyed, such as riding horses. He was a boost to my morale as I had begun to feel so unattractive and uncared for. His only failing was he had a drinking problem, and he would be drunk by the end of the date. Finally, one week-end evening he had been drinking too much and was driving in the country when his car ran off the road and into a large pond. He managed to wade out of the water and walked to a house and called me at two in the morning to come get him. I woke Seth up and the two of us made the 30- mile trip to the pond to pick him up. On that ride through the country side, I started thinking about our relationship. He was a drinker, like my dad had been, so I knew that was not a good environment in which to raise a child. Also, he had been married three times. That fact brought a memory back from my father's family that taunted me since we had started dating. My dad had a brother that had been married 5 times. My mother was talking to my dad's mother, Grand-mother Constantine, regarding this son who was contemplating his 6th marriage. Grandmother Constantine said to my mother, "I just don't understand why he can't find a good woman." My mother replied "Grandma, 5 women can't be wrong." I took this to heart and decided I didn't want to be number 4.

That relationship ended, and I dated three other men from my past who were divorced. One of them was home from the Navy and proposed to me on the first date. I never dated him again. Near Christmas, I was invited by a friend, who had never been married to attend a wedding. He was the same one I had attended the New Year's party with while I was on "leave" from the Sanatorium. We went to the wedding and had a great time. I was very fond of him and saw him a few more times before he had to return to college.

During that December month, I was sitting at a local drive-in restaurant, visiting with my friend, Janie, who I worked with at the bank, and her boyfriend. They were both concerned that I had not found anyone I liked to date. I told her I did not want anyone who had been married before or was a heavy drinker. And I would like for him to be taller than me, as I was 5'8" and liked to wear high heels on a date. She said to her boyfriend, "How about your friend, Buddy?" Before he got a chance to answer, I said "That sounds like a dog's name," and immediately I regretted what I had said. I blurted out, "Sorry, I just am not a friend of nicknames, but I like unusual names." Well, Janie said "If you like unusual names, how about Adrian Molenaar?" I said, "Yes, is he tall?" visualizing this foreign looking man, with a little moustache. She said, "Yes," and she would arrange a blind date. She was to check if he was available for a Christmas party they were planning to attend the following Friday. She called later and told me to be ready at 7pm. They would bring him and pick me up for the party.

This was the first date I had with someone I did not previously know. I was nervous and put on a cranberry wool skirt with a velvet cranberry top and cranberry patent shoes. I then put on a gold necklace and earrings. I had put my blond hair up in what they called a "beehive" and thought I looked pretty sophisticated for a country girl. The doorbell rang and when I opened the door, there stood Janie and a partially balding man who came up to my nose. I said, "This is Adrian?" and she said, "No, Adrian had something else he had to do tonight and couldn't come. This is Douglas." As we were walking to the car, I was trying to act as though I was not disappointed so to appear gracious to this young man, who was my date. This was not easy.

When we arrived at the party, I discovered it was a company party and did not know that my blind date, Adrian had sent his employee to that party. The next day he told Adrian, "What a mistake, you should have gone out with that girl." He described me to Adrian and later that week, Adrian called me and asked me on a double-date, the week before Christmas. He apologized for not being able to come to the first date. I accepted his excuse and the night of the date came and I wore the same cranberry outfit again. When I opened the door this time, there stood a 6'4" man in cowboy boots and a Stetson hat. All I could think of when I saw him was, he certainly does not look like a Frenchman, and I do not like that style hat on him. We went to the restaurant, which was a dance club, and he asked me to dance. When we got on the dance floor, he said it was wonderful to be with a woman that was tall enough to look him in the face, when we danced. I thought it was great to dance with someone who was not shorter than me.

On the way home, I discovered that his father, like mine was a farm equipment dealer and had come here from Holland. Adrain was named after his uncle in Belgium. No Frenchman here! He also told me that he was on his way to New Orleans for the Sugar Bowl on New Years Day. He asked if I would like to go. There were two reasons that I had to tell him no. First, I was working at the bank and could not get time off. The major reason was, I was using any surplus money to pay off a local department store for the expensive clothes my ex had charged and refused to pay. My name was on that account also so I didn't want to ruin my credit. I needed what I had to support my son and me. I thanked him and said I would see him when he got back. I think he was shocked that I said, "No."

When my father heard about the trip, he said he wanted me to go and he would pay for it. I told him "I would not chase a man to New Orleans and take a chance of losing my job. If he truly is interested in me, he'll be back." Daddy and Mother were not getting along very well, and I suspected that my new car had a lot to do with it. After all, it had been his decision to give me the home, not hers and she had told me recently that if I ever married, they wanted the house back. If my parents had not given me that home as a gift, I would not be able to make enough to survive and pay rent. I did not want to press my luck and start having Daddy subsidize me on frivolous things, like trips. Daddy had made the comment when I moved in with them for the divorce, that I never had to leave, as he would help support me forever. Now I could tell he had grown tired of honoring that remark, and was pushing me to find the right kind of husband. The eye-catching car was acting as "bait" and the trip with Adrian to the bowl game was a dead giveaway that he thought he might be the one.

Sure enough, when Adrian came back, he called me and we went out to the movie that week end. Before, I tell you this story about us, I need to let you know that my father never cussed in front of me (except in the case of a "slip up" or he did not know I could hear him). He also never told dirty jokes. We went to the movie, sat down and Adrian started holding my hand. During the previews of the new movies, a picture of a dog appeared and my love for this animal became obvious. I said to Adrian, "What a cute dog." He said, "I have a dog." I said, "What kind is he?" to which he answered, "I'm not sure, but he has a split personality." I said, "Really, I never heard of a dog with that problem." To which he said, "He hates cats but loves pussy." I yanked my hand out of his and straightened up in my chair. I was embarrassed by this joke. I could tell by his face, that he was sorry he had said it. We sat through the whole movie without speaking to each other. Afterwards, when we got to the car, he said, "I'm sorry, I didn't mean to offend you. Can we still go out to eat?" I accepted the apology and dinner would be nice since I was really hungry, so I said, "Yes."

The next time we had a date, he dropped in another bad joke and when I got home, I thought I'm not going out with him again. But then he called to ask if he could take Seth and me out on Sunday afternoon to eat lunch. We went out and it was love at first sight for my son and Adrian. Adrian loved to play with my 3- year old child, and Seth loved the attention. I had gotten Seth's hair cut like the young John Kennedy and he looked adorable and different. Almost all of the little boys had a flat top or a buzzed haircut like their daddy's. After that I could see the bond between the two of them, we began to date regularly.

I had not heard from my ex-husband, since the divorce. One Friday night, Adrian and I were invited to an engagement party. I rushed home from work to get ready to go. Mother was keeping Seth, and I called her to ask if she would bring my shoes that I had left at her house. I told her not to hurry, as I was going to jump in the shower right now. I hung up the phone undressed, showered and as soon as I stepped out, I heard the back door bell ringing. I thought I must have accidentally locked the door, and my mother was already here. There was nothing but a small towel so I wrapped it around me. You could not see out the back door, so I threw it open, and there stood Adrian and my ex-husband! The towel did not cover me adequately, so I slammed the door in their faces. I thought, "My God, Adrian thinks I'm still seeing my ex-husband, while my ex-husband thinks I'm seeing Adrian like this in front of my child. I put a robe on and went back to the door to find my mother was there, also. I turned to my ex who said," I just had some papers I needed you to sign as I've been drafted." I said, "Fine, I will leave them at your mother's house tomorrow." I took them out of his hand. He turned and walked to his car without looking back. That was the last time I saw my ex for 11 years. I told Mother and Adrian to come in. After Mother left, Adrian said, "I'm sorry I was early but I had the wrong time. Is there something going on with you and your ex?" I explained to him what had happened, and he laughed, then said, "Why did you slam the door in our faces?" I said, "Because I was shocked and embarrassed. I didn't have another option, since the towel was not adequate to cover everything." He hugged me and said, "Miss Modesty."

We dated until July, 1966 when he asked me to marry him. He pulled up to the house to pick me up for dinner and said, would you get me my sunglasses out of the glove box, please. When I opened the glove box, there were two diamond rings facing me. I was delighted to see the beautiful emerald cut solitaire and another large round solitaire diamond that he was offering me. He said, "I couldn't make up my mind so I brought you two choices." I was astounded! Both rings were beautiful and we spent the weekend celebrating our engagement in St. Louis. I wore one on each hand the whole weekend. The emerald cut ended up being the winner.

I was not in a rush to remarry since it had only been 7 months since my divorce. I said, "Yes, both Seth and I would be happy to marry you." The whole time I was looking at these rings and wondering how he could have afforded them. I later found out he had sold his beloved 1931 Chevrolet, 4- door. He had spent most of his teenage years restoring this unique car that looked like something that belonged to Al Capone's "Mob." We finally made plans to marry in early 1967, but his father was diagnosed with cancer in the fall of 1966, so we set our marriage aside for a later date so as not to put a damper on the joyous occasion.

CHAPTER 37

ADRIAN'S MOTHER'S CONSPIRACY

In February, 1967, Adrain's father died leaving him the responsibility of managing the farm equipment business, where he had been working. Now he was the sole support of his mother. His twin sister was teaching school in Germany and had come home to be with her father until his death. Now she was returning to Europe, and his mother did not want Adrian to leave home. I knew that his father was very fond of me and was excited about the marriage. His mother was opposed to our marriage, because I was a divorcee, and they were Catholic.

Adrian suggested that I consider joining the church. There was a young priest in a small town near us and we went to visit with him. We liked him a lot, so I began taking lessons to join. He had told us possibly we could work out a dispensation, and if I had finished the lessons, we could marry in the church immediately after it was received. His Mother had suggested that we also visit with the Monsignor at his home parish about a dispensation and marriage. We did as she suggested and visited the local parish first.

What we did not know was his mother had contacted a friend of hers, who had a lot of influence with the local church.

This woman was going to ask the Monsignor to discourage the marriage and not offer to help get a dispensation for us. (A dispensation was an appeal to the Pope by your church for us to be exempted from a specific Canon law. In this case, we needed to have this previous marriage dissolved, and the Monsignor would help us to find a correct method suitable to attain the dispensation.) Without this dispensation, Adrian would be unable to receive communion from the church. He had always been a faithful participant in the Catholic Church, and communion was extremely important to him.

We made our appointment and went to the Rectory. The Monsignor was very cordial when he opened the door as we followed him into his office. He asked us to be seated and immediately asked why we were there. Adrian told him all the details about our meeting and how we had come to seek a dispensation, so that I might join the church and be married by a priest.

He became very silent, and he looked at me, then turned to Adrian. He said, "What do you see in this woman whose body has been violated by another man?" We both were so shocked at this crude remark! I could feel the heat coming into my face and did not know if it was from embarrassment or shock! Adrian was silent, then he looked at me and said, "Let's go, I'm finished here." The Monsignor, who all of a sudden appeared very "flustered" immediately stood up, and blurted, "There are ways of getting dispensations, but they are expensive and take a long time." Adrian said, "I'm not buying my way into my own church." He grabbed me by the hand, then we stood up and walked out the door. We got in the car and I could tell how upset he was so I said "I'm sorry." He said, "Lydia, I'm the one who is sorry to have exposed you to someone who hurt and embarrassed you. I'll not ask the church again."

We went back to my house. I called and told the young priest who had been giving me the lessons, that I could not continue and explained the reason. I could tell by the tone of his voice that this upset him, so I thanked him and concluded the conversation as quickly as possible. I only lacked one lesson being through, so I understood a lot of good things about the church now, even if they didn't want me.

It was a sad night for both of us and he drove home early. The first thing he said, when I heard from Adrian the next day, was that he was going to continue to attend church. You understand that after we marry, I cannot take communion. I said "I do not want to stand between you and your beliefs." Adrian said, "I still have my beliefs, but I love you, and I'm going to marry you.

My deceased father-in-law, Jan who was very fond of me had a best friend, named Alec who was a widower. He had confided in Alec about his wife's conspiracy with the church. He knew what his wife was doing. He had told Alec that he knew his son wanted to marry me, and he had asked Alec to do anything he could to see that it happened. Jan's death changed everything. The following month, Alec called me and asked if I could come by his office after work. When I entered the room, he stood up and closed the door behind me. After asking me to sit down, he immediately began to tell me what he had been asked to do. He said, "Lydia, when are you and Adrian planning to marry?" I said, "I don't know now, because Adrian said that his mother was so distraught about his father dying, and with his sister leaving so soon for Europe, it doesn't make for an ideal time."

I told Alec that Adrian's mother told him she was fearful of being left alone and needed his companionship for a while until she improved. Alec said "How long have you dated him?" I said "About two years." He said "That's too long! Are you or are you not giving him any?" I said, "That's an embarrassing question!" He said, "Well, I'm just trying to come up with some way to put some pressure on him to marry. Here's another idea." "I'll plan a party for the two of you and make the announcement of your marriage date. Let's pick one out." I said, "Because of Lent, Catholics have to marry after Easter." He said, "April 15th is the first Saturday after Easter, we'll use that one. I promised Jan I would not let Adrian's mother attempt to keep this marriage from happening and I'm a man of my word." Then he explained to me about what had transpired between his mother and her friend to try and end Adrian and my relationship.

I was flabbergasted at this hurtful thing that his mother had done to us, and Alec's intervention. I told him that I thought Adrian would balk and take his mother's side, because he was so kind-hearted and wanted to make everybody happy. I could see he respected her, but was not the type to stand his ground against her. Alec said, "I want you to go by his office and tell him you are tired of waiting for this marriage to happen and give him his engagement ring back. Leave immediately and go to the movie out of town or someplace he would not think to look for you for at least 4 hours. Then go to your father's house and wait." I was concerned that we might never be married, as his mother had such a strong hold on him, so I agreed to do it.

I drove up to Adrian's business and walked in. The secretary and one of his employees were in the front office. I spoke to everyone, then asked Adrian to come outside. I took the ring off and handed it to him. I said, "Adrian I'm tired of waiting for you to agree on a date for us to marry. I want to find a husband and a father for Seth, and I need that kind of life now. I'm sorry, it's over." His face told it all. He couldn't come up with a word and I said nothing more, got in the car and left.

I went to a town 30 miles away and went to the movie. I was so apprehensive that I cannot tell you what the movie was about. Afterwards, I drove home and went by my father's house and Adrian's car was parked in the drive. I went to my house and called my dad. He said, "Lydia, you need to come over here as Adrian is here and very upset about your break-up." "What does he have to say about it?", I asked. "He says he loves you and Seth so he wants both of you to be his family." I agreed to come by the house and talk about it. I walked in the door, and Seth came running to me. He was crying so I picked him up and went into another room. I said "Seth, what is the matter? He said, 'Now you've ruined everything! You broke up with Adrian and now I'll never have a brother!" I laughed and said, 'Let's go see Adrian and see If we can fix it." I sat down on the sofa, facing Adrian while Seth jumped in his lap.

We reconciled. I told Daddy and Adrian about Alec, and what he had said. Daddy said, "Adrian, you and I have one thing in common. We both love Lydia and Seth so we want the best for them. I agree with Alec, you need to marry now, before your mother gets accustomed to having you there by her side, permanently."

Adrian went home and his sister was packing to return to Europe. When he told her what had happened and that he was going to get married right away, she said she was going to stay in the states until after the ceremony. She has always been an advocate of mine and like the sister I never had. He told his mother he was getting married on the 15th of April. Her response was that if we married, she certainly would not come to the wedding. He said "Mother, if you don't come, you will never see me again." She said nothing and he went upstairs to his room.

Alec was a man of his word and had a catered cocktail party in our honor to announce the day of our wedding. April 15, 1967, the first Saturday after Easter. Adrian had a Catholic childhood friend who spent the evening talking to Adrian's mother and causing her to weep off and on, into her handkerchief. He was loud enough that I could hear him talking about how our marriage would never last, and Adrian would be sorry he had deserted the church, etc. I kept smiling and trying to keep up a good front, as I didn't want everyone there to know how his mother felt about our marriage. I finally walked into the bar area where Alec's son in law, who was very pleased that Adrian and I were marrying, was standing. He said "Don't pay any attention to that jealous son of a bitch. He treats his wife terrible and thinks that he can make Adrain's life miserable like hers. He enjoys feeling superior to his friends, is all wrapped up in himself and always will be." I was so shocked by what he had to say. I was an outsider in this town and I just wanted to be able to get along with Adrian's friends. This opened up to a whole new group of people that I wasn't really acquainted with.

One of the few true friends we had at that time, was a couple named Denton. Tim Denton had been a friend of Adrian's since childhood. Just a year before he had married a girl from out of town, named Julie. The first time I saw her, I thought she was the most beautiful girl I had ever seen. She was a striking brunette with flawless skin, a wonderful figure and a sweet disposition that never changed. Now she was pregnant and very large as she was getting close to delivery. We had become friends with the other girls in town, but Julie and I were closer, possibly because we were the two new out of towners. The other couple we were friends with was the son and daughter in law of Alec. Alec's family had just lived one door down from Adrian's family. Scott was a very witty and fun person to be around and always mischievous. His wife, Paula was a very petite, pretty and perky blond with an always happy attitude that made you like her immediately. We didn't know it then, but these 2 couples would be our friends for life.

CHAPTER 38

MARRIED AGAIN

The month soon ran away with us, with Mother taking me to the city to buy a dress. I picked a pale blue Alencon lace dress and jacket, with a bow at the neck with matching shoes. Adrian selected a dark suit, white shirt and a tie. He had lost weight and looked very handsome. He had let his curly hair grow a little longer, and this added to his looks. I selected a yellow rose corsage instead of a bouquet to be purchased by Adrian. His mother and sister selected gardenia corsages. The wedding would be at my parent's house with yellow rose floral arrangements, assorted hors d'oeuvre, cake and ice cream. It would be only close friends and relatives, and in the morning, as we had to go to Memphis, to catch a plane to New Orleans for our honeymoon.

My friends at the bank where I worked gave me a wedding shower. I will never forget when Julie walked into the wedding shower wearing house slippers. Her feet were so swollen she couldn't wear regular shoes. The Doctor had told her it was going to be a few more weeks before the baby would be there. My mother-in-law to be who had twins, told her she was going to have twins. Julie said, "No mam. The doctor said there is only one baby!" I could have hugged Julie's neck for coming. How many others might have said, "I can't go, I don't have any shoes to wear. I look so swollen that I don't want people to see me." What a true friend! And always has been.

The night before the wedding, April 14th, Tim who was to be our best man, called to say he had taken Julie to the hospital with labor pains, and that we should get another best man for the next day. Adrian got on the phone and called another childhood friend to take Tim's place. My matron of honor, Janie was the friend from the bank who had introduced me to Adrian. We had been fast friends from the time I started working with her. She was a very sincere woman, and I had just been her bridesmaid, the past year.

Early on the day of the wedding, my phone rang. It was Adrian telling me that Tim and Julie had twin girls! What a surprise for her, but not for my mother-in-law. She reminded Julie for the rest of her life that she was right. Adrian and I were excited and sorry that we were leaving town, as we were anxious to see the baby girls.

I went to my parents' house early, to wait for everyone to come and to help mother with the food and decorations. A Judge was going to marry us. We selected him in case we got a dispensation later. Not being married in another church would make it an easier transition. When Adrian's family arrived, I could tell that he was a nervous wreck. His mother and sister had on their gardenias. His other turned and said to Adrian, "Where are Lydia's roses?" He had that "deer in the headlight" look! He said "I forgot them." I could tell he was upset. It did not upset me at all. Mother seemed unusually happy, which was very odd. I thought maybe she is glad, as this meant we would never be coming back to live with them. My thoughts told me that she would be unhappy because we were moving to another town. She would no longer be baby- sitting Seth. She certainly had tried to spend every hour she could with him and I wanted both my parents to have a good relationship with my child. He was staying with them while we went on the honeymoon.

After seeking a corsage for me by calling the local florist, Adrian was "blue," when he found out they were closed on Saturday. His Mother said to me, "Come here Lydia, I'd like for you to wear my gardenias." Before I could say a word, she had pinned them on me. I could smell the sweet aroma rising up from the delicate blooms. She squeezed my hand and I felt like she was trying to apologize. I smiled at her and said, "Thank you, they smell wonderful." Adrian and I joined hands, and his hands were so sweaty and clammy, I felt sorry for him. It was obvious that he was very nervous. When the Judge said, "You may kiss the bride, Adrian put his arms around me and gave me a wonderful kiss! In a matter of a few minutes, I was married again! I prayed silently and said, "Dear Lord, please don't let this be a mistake. He's a wonderful man, but he will have so much to endure from his mother and his church for marrying me."

While everyone was visiting and taking pictures, my new sister-in-law, along with another wild and fun friend, Jewel and one of Adrian's employees had started working on our car. They had taken the wheels off of my Mustang so we couldn't drive it and painted Adrian's new car with white shoe polish. "Honk at the Newlyweds, Hot Springs tonight," and other things that were not so nice were in large letters. There were tin cans and shoes attached to the back. As we got into the car to leave, I looked up at the most beautiful spring day of my life. The temperature was perfect, the sky was cloudless, and the trees were all budding out in my parent's large yard. I had every reason to be happy and I truly was! When he got into the car, covered with rice and good wishes, and drove away, he said, "Lydia, I love you and am proud to have you for my wife." I said, "I am proud to have you, too."

A few miles down the road, we had lost the cans and shoes. Everybody on the road was honking at us, which was fun for a while. However, we didn't want to enter the city where the airport was with all this stuff on the car.

We held hands for several miles, when suddenly he turned off the road. He headed to a service station. I said, "Are we out of gas?" He said, "No, I want to get this shoe polish off my car. Two attendants came out with hoses, and I stood by Adrian as they soaped the car and tried to remove the polish. I looked at the big sign on the side of the car that said, "Hot Springs Tonight." I turned to Adrian and said, "That's a silly sign. We're not going to Hot Springs, we're going to New Orleans." His eyes rolled up and he was smiling. The two attendants both turned around and looked at me and then at each other.

When we got into the car Adrian said, "Lydia, the sign meant we were going to make the springs in the bed hot and had nothing to do with our destination." I told him I hope we never stopped at that station again because it had embarrassed me. They probably thought, "What a dumb blond." Then we both laughed. The polish would never come off the car entirely, so we ended up having to trade it later.

New Orleans was a wonderful place for a honeymoon. We had perfect weather and the food was wonderful. Our hotel room was a corner room that looked out over the swimming pool and gorgeous courtyard. Finally, it was time to go home and we were at the end of our money. Few people had credit cards in 1967, so Adrian was carrying cash. We knew what we needed to pay for the room and had saved ten dollars over that amount to pay our way out of the parking garage in Memphis. When we went down to pay, the desk clerk said that was not enough money, because there were special taxes for hotels in New Orleans.

Adrian and I talked about what to do. I had my checkbook from my bank where I had worked for the past two years. I knew every person there. I told Adrian the desk clerk said they would take a check, but would have to call our bank to verify the check would clear. Adrian said, "How much money do you have in that account?" I said "about $5.00." He said, "And you think they are going to let you write a check for this large amount with $5.00 dollars to cover it." I said, "Maybe." Adrian had money in his account at another bank but did not have a checkbook with him, so this was our best bet. Joan was head of the bookkeeping department and very strict and this was a large check. At that time Adrian was making $90.00 a week and I was making $60.00. The bookkeeping department was composed of most of the friends who gave the shower. I knew they would help if they could.

I stepped up to the counter and using all of my 23- year- old bravado, I said to the desk clerk, "If you call my bank and ask for the bookkeeping department, a lady named Joan can tell you if the check will clear." The clerk dialed the bank and asked for the bookkeeping department. She said "This is the Vieux Carre Hotel in New Orleans. I have a check from a Lydia Constantine, who has an account with your bank and wants to pay her bill to us. I need to know if she has enough money in her account to clear this check." Joan asked what the amount was, and I was so nervous. Adrian was sitting in a lobby chair watching to see how this turned out.

I had no other option if she said no, and I knew Joan would have to lie If she said yes. Her reputation for honesty and perfection was being "put to the test." There was a slight period of silence, while Joan checked the account. She came back to the phone and the clerk said yes, thank you and hung up the phone. I thought I might faint before she got around to telling me the decision. She looked sternly at me and said, the bank says you can write a check for any amount you ceem necessary. I turned to look at Adrain and smiled. What a relief! I wrote the check and handed it to the clerk. She gave me the receipt without a single word said. My bank didn't let me down that day and they're still our banker, 58 years later.

The next day I was back at work with Adrian's check in my

hand to deposit. I hurried down to the bookkeeping department to thank Joan for approving the check. I told her I had already made the deposit. When I walked in everyone applauded! Joan laughed and said, "I was afraid if we didn't pay it, we might have to come to New Orleans to bail you two out of jail for non-payment." I hugged her and thanked everyone for helping me out of the problem and went back upstairs to work in the loan department.

Adrian and I had rented a house in a middle- class neighborhood. Even though my parents had given me the house I had been living in which was near them. Adrian wanted them to sell it and we would rent and buy a home ourselves when we could afford it. I was okay with that, but we had a hard time finding a home because rentals didn't like families with children. They would gladly take a dog or cat, but not a child, which I found strange.

CHAPTER 39

MOTHER AND DADDY TRY TO TAKE CONTROL

About three months after moving in, my parents had sold my house near them. They came to visit. Seth was excited to see them and after playing around with him for a few minutes, Daddy sat down on the couch followed by Mother. After she was seated, he said, "I want you two to hear me through. I have brought some money from the sale of the house. I want you two to find a house, and we will give you the down payment as a wedding gift. You are wasting money when you rent, and if you are paying for a house, you're building equity for your future and Seths. I looked at Adrian and he said, "May we give you a decision tomorrow?" They said yes and shortly afterwards they left for home.

When they left Adrian said, "I know you want the money for a different house. I never liked the situation you had at the other house where your mother had a key to the house. She never knocked before she came in. If you will agree to not giving your house key to her, I will accept the gift. I said, "That would be fine." and we called them the next morning. We moved to a better part of town next to a railroad track. It was small but new with a basement and was in the school district that we wanted for Seth. We spent the next seven years in that house.

Shortly after we moved in, I discovered that I was pregnant again. Seth was 5 years old and excited about the new baby. I knew that my bank job would be over when I started showing, because that was a policy of banks and a lot of other businesses to ask you to go home (with no pay) when that occurred. For some reason they did not want the public to see you. If you had a bookkeeping job you could stay on because they worked in the basement, and no one could see them but the other employees.

I took care of the loan department, serving as a secretary, preparing loans and collecting payments from customers. I also processed every customer's information that they used for income tax purposes. I had started this job the moment the bank had moved into its new facility. This was a new department, and I was the first to run it. I had been hired from another company specifically for this purpose. All the loan officers were also in this location.

I conceived in August and by the first of March, 1968, I was preparing for my last days at work. The end of the first week was my last day. I went home and started preparing the baby's room and doing all the "nest building" that all expectant mothers do when delivery is getting close.

About a week later, I received a call from the bank. The loan department head told me that they needed me to come back to work as long as I could. The customers were coming in wanting their tax information papers. No one knew how to do them, because it had always been my job, and they had not trained anyone else. I said, "I am really showing now so I can't come back." He said, "We're going to make an office in the basement for you. I replied, "All my heavy files are in that area where I work and I will have to be upstairs or I'm not coming back." He said, "They will never allow that." I said "Then find someone else to do this job or ask them if I can come back." The next morning, he called to say I could work upstairs. All the women loved the change. The third week of March, I came back and all the customers were so kind and excited about the baby and totally unaware that I had been expecting when I left. The bank was pleased that some of the customers had told them how advanced our bank was to allow me to work while "showing."

I worked until April the 15th getting all the information together for everyone. Then I went home to stay. By that time, I looked like I might explode! I was not a Feminist but I felt I had struck a blow for the women in our area with my being able to work while pregnant.

CHAPTER 40

OUR FAMILY GROWS

In May 1968, I gave birth to an 8 pounds 7 ounce boy, with red hair. When Adrian took me to the hospital, they were doing remodeling, so I had to be put in a labor room with another mother to be. She was expecting triplets, and it was too early for them to come. They were giving her meds to stop the labor. She was by herself, crying, yelling and having a horrible time getting comfortable. Adrian had been sitting with me for an hour or so then and said, "I'm going downstairs to get a drink, I'll be right back." I believe he was leaving for a reprieve from the yelling as much as for a drink. As he got up, my roommate ceased her noise and said to him, "Hey, while you're down there, would you bring me back a funny book?" Adrian could not look at me, because I saw he was about to burst into laughter. He said, "Do you mean a comic book?" "Yeah, an Archie or a Batman," she said. I was lying there having labor pains and trying to figure out how anyone, that acted in such pain, could put their pain aside to read a "funny book."

My mother hated red hair so she always colored hers brown. She was not as elated with the birth of another red head like we were. He had beautiful blue eyes and was the best baby. He drank the whole 4 ounce bottle the first time they brought him to me. Quite different from Seth who would only take 2 ounces every 4 hours. When he went home, he immediately started sleeping all night. We named him Caleb. I adored him and his brother but I thought I was finished having babies. As he grew, he developed curls and his red hair faded to a golden blond. He was very fair, so it was hard to keep him from burning in the sun. His complexion was the kind that a lot of women would pay a fortune to obtain.

CHAPTER 41

MY HEART IS BROKEN

A few weeks later, we were getting used to our new baby. Spring had come and the back of our new house had a place perfect to plant a garden. Adrian had helped me work it up, so while Seth was taking a nap, I placed Caleb in the crib by the patio window. That way, I could keep an eye on him while I worked. I was on my knees planting onions when I heard someone pull into the drive. I got up and stepped around the corner. There was my dad, by himself, stepping out of the truck. He had never visited me without Mother in attendance. I became very anxious, as I could tell by his demeanor that something was wrong.

His first words were, "Lydia, can we talk for a few minutes?" I said, "Certainly, it's such a nice day why don't we sit on the patio as Caleb is in the crib by the door and Seth is taking a nap? He sat down and said, "I won't take up much of your time as I wanted to visit with you, while Seth was asleep. So, I'll get right to it." He said, "Lydia, I have something special to talk to you about. I know you only have ½ year of college and would like to finish your education. I know how much money you and Adrian have to live on. I want to offer you an opportunity to finish your degree. Your mother and I will fund it". I was so excited and said,

"That's wonderful, I would love to do that. Adrian and I could pay you back yearly, as soon as I get finished." He said, "I do not want you to pay it back, I have a better idea." I said "You know that Adrian will not take the money if we can't pay it back."

Daddy became red in the face! I couldn't decide if he was mad or embarrassed. He blurted out these words that I will never forget! "Your mother and I want Seth. That's all she can talk about. You have another son now, and we can afford to support Seth. He will have everything he needs in life. You and Adrian don't have enough money to support one child, let alone two. Your mother had a cruel step-father, and she cannot bear the thought of Seth having a step-father. Adrian is nice now, but in the future, he might turn out to be like your mother's step-father. You need this education to succeed in life. Do you realize what a wonderful opportunity this is?" With that he pulled some rolled up papers out of his jacket. He said, "I've brought the paperwork with me for you to sign and we will legally adopt Seth and change his name to ours. You can come see him whenever you want, but he will belong to us."

I felt as though I had been slapped in the face and my mind was conjuring up all kinds of answers to these questions, but instead I said, "What kind of Mother do you think I am, that would give up my child for money? He is mine and I love him! Adrian loves Seth as much as I do and we'd rather starve than give up a child. I have always allowed Seth to be with the two of you, even though mother always acts as though he is hers not mine, anyway! Why do you need possession? I thought Seth would make up for that boy you expected, when I was born. This hateful scheme sounds just like Mother. I hope in your heart that you would never have thought of a plan to do this to me, Daddy. If you did, you have certainly done a lot of faking about how much you loved me. Was the help with the house and the joy of hearing I had another boy, all part of your plan to get me out of your life, and take my son? Did the two of you think that as long as I had another son to love, I'd be delighted to hand Seth over to you. Well, you're wrong and I don't care if I ever see the two of you again."

I never cry because I am unhappy, only when I am unusually mad. This was one of those moments! I suppose my yelling had awakened the baby, as he began to cry about the same time. I opened the door and my tears were so thick that I could barely see through them. I picked up the baby and walked into the house and locked the door behind me. Daddy knocked on the door but I didn't answer. I finally heard him start the truck to leave and I was relieved. I tried to pull myself together because in a little while Seth would be getting up from his nap, and I didn't want him to see me crying.

I thought what kind of parents do I have? How cruel can they be? I didn't call Adrian at work because I wanted to calm down before he came home. Instead, I called Mother's sister, Aunt Ann and told her what had happened. She and my mother were so close. She started to make excuses for Mother and then she changed her mind and said, "Lydia, I'm sorry but this time they crossed over the line. I'm going to have a serious talk with her about apologizing, as I don't want the family to break up. Before I do, you and Adrian need to tell me if you are willing to accept an apology?" I told her that as this moment I wasn't but would like a week or two to visit with Adrian about it.

When Adrian walked in the door that night, he could tell I was upset. I had sent Seth over to play with the next- door neighbor's child as I did not want him to witness this traumatic mess. My eyes were red and swollen. Adrian sat down by me on the sofa, put his arms around me and in between sobbing and telling him what happened the tears kept flowing until I was so choked up, I couldn't talk anymore. I cried until I went to bed and could not go to sleep because I was so congested. It was over two weeks, before we heard from them. Daddy called and told both of us that they had make a terrible mistake. Mother finally came to the phone and asked me if they could see Seth. I knew how much Seth loved them so I said, "Yes." She hung up the phone with no apology.

Adrian said, "I want to adopt Seth and change his name. I'll talk to him about it." When he told Seth he jumped in Adrian's lap and hugged him. Seth was excited, but not as excited as Adrian! I had not asked for child support, but it had been awarded to me by the Judge anyway. My ex was now in the army, and if he had told them he had a child, we would have received money on a regular basis. I had been divorced over three years, and he had never sent a penny to Seth. Adrian and I talked to a lawyer who said since my ex had never sent money for Seth's support, the court would probably assume that was desertion. She thought it would be fairly easy for Adrian to adopt him. We applied and soon Seth belonged to us both.

CHAPTER 42

ILLNESS INTRUDES AGAIN

At the beginning of the second year of Caleb's life, he developed a breathing problem. I had taken him to the emergency room 2 or 3 times with the croup. When he was 16 months old, one night around 11pm, his breathing became labored, and he developed a croup. I woke Adrian. We took Caleb and Seth in their pajamas and headed to the emergency room. Half way there, Caleb's little head fell into my lap and I thought he was dead! I was hysterical! The minute we arrived Adrian grabbed his limp body and jumped out of the car running into the ER. I retrieved Seth. They took him into a room and gave him some medication which appeared to be reviving him. I was crying uncontrollably, and his Pediatrician, Dr. Jones was trying to calm me down.

He said, "Lydia, I believe you need to take this child to an Allergist in the city. These episodes are becoming more serious each time I see him. He is the youngest I have ever seen that had this serious a problem. He needs to be tested. This is Thursday and I want him to be somewhere Monday. I'll find you an allergist."

True to his word, Dr. Jones found us a pediatric allergist. On

Monday, I was on the way to the Allergist in Memphis, TN, with my baby boy and Adrian's Mother. I had asked my mother to go with me, first and she said she would keep Seth. We were to stay until all the tests were concluded, so perhaps it would give her additional time to enjoy Seth.

Dr. Crowell was the one we had the appointment with and he had a wonderful bedside manner. He ran a few tests the first day, and Caleb showed positive on some of them. He decided he needed a full allergy panel in order to pin down what truly was causing the problem. Every day for the next 3 days, he had a battery of needle pricks which made him cry. It hurt me, every time one was administered. After he had had the final ones, he had several small allergies show up. The strongest ones were mildew and mold. We lived in a fairly new home so it was hard to imagine we would have a mold problem. They gave him his first allergy shot and sent us home with the serum he would have to have injected.

It was suggested we should take the rug up in his room, remove the curtains and any other cloth items that might harbor mildew or mold. All of this was done, and the following week we had another trip to the emergency room. These spells always were after 11pm at night. One of my mother-in-law's friends, Mrs. Long was a retired biology teacher and had come to visit her. She was telling Mrs. Long about the problem of not being able to locate the source of the mold and mildew. Mrs. Long said, "I'll go home and get some petri dishes and put a medium in them then we'll place them all over the house where mold and mildew might grow. I believe this will find your source." She came back to our house and placed the dishes under the sinks, all over the bathroom and in the kitchen and through- out the house. When she got to Caleb's room, she placed them all over the room and in the window sills. Several days later, she came back and retrieved them all.

When Mrs. Long gave us her report, it showed the twin bed that Caleb had been moved into out of his crib had large amounts of mold and some mildew growing in every dish that was near the bed. The twin bed had come from an unheated storage room at my mother-in-law's house. It apparently had mold on the inside but did not have any odor. We immediately removed it and bought a new bed. The spells he had been having were coming only at night after he had been put to bed and had inhaled the fumes for a few hours. By 11pm, he had inhaled all his body could take.

I wish I could tell you that this was the end of the problem, but I think he must have had respiratory problems aggravated by the mold. He had to have allergy shots monthly, and Dr. Crowell continued to see him every 6 weeks. We would drive to Memphis to get a check-up and the refill on his allergy medication. Dr. Crowell also rigged up a bicycle pump with a nebulizer on it for us to use for him to inhale. I would pump the pump as though I was inflating a bicycle tire, and he would inhale as I did it. It was important to do this immediately when he had a "spell." He continued to have ER trips until he was a teenager, and finally they became less frequent. We rarely let him stay overnight with friends because we were afraid that he would have a "spell" then no one would understand what to do with the bicycle pump. If that happened, he would pass out and possibly die.

I sometime worried that Caleb's problems had come from me since I had the weak lung system in the family. I was afraid that his lungs might be weakened and susceptible to Tuberculosis. Children with asthma and other respiratory problems are always a worry for their parents.

Caleb began to improve from allergy problems and by the beginning of 1970, was much healthier. His brother was in school so things were a little less hectic for me. I could sleep better at night knowing we wouldn't be making that trip to the

ER at 11PM. I had developed a pattern of waking every hour and checking on him to make sure he wasn't starting the croup again. Fortunately, I was able to lay back down and fall asleep immediately each time. It was hard to break myself of this habit.

CHAPTER 43

GETTING TO KNOW OUR FAMILY BETTER

Our sons were quite a joy to us and as they grew, they did a lot of those things that most parents say, "I wish I had written that down." I'm sharing some of those things I did write down."

When Seth was small, about 4 years old, we were taking a little walk when we came upon a few ants on the sidewalk. Seth was trying to walk around them when he stepped on one or two. He started crying. I asked, "Why are you crying?" He said, "Dad told me don't kill anything unless you plan to eat it. I don't want to eat those ants!" I explained to him that dad was talking about wild game, not insects. He was so relieved.

Adrian was easily distracted when he was baby- sitting the boys. I ran to the store once, and he had Caleb in the yard with him when he was about 2 years old. He said, "You go on. I'll keep him until you get back." When I came back with the groceries, I was unloading them, and I yelled at Adrian for help. He was chatting with the neighbor across our fence. I stepped into the house and I said, "Where's Caleb?" He said, "He's riding his little duck in the yard." (The duck was on four wheels and had handles on its head so Caleb could ride it while pushing it forward with his feet.) I ran out in the yard to look for him and

Adrian ran around the front of the house. Caleb was nowhere in sight! I ran into the house to call the police and heard the phone ringing. When I answered it was my next-door neighbor. She said, "Lydia, Caleb is down by the elementary school riding his duck on the boulevard!" That was about 3 blocks away! I jumped in the car and took off after him. He was nearly to the school when I pulled off to catch him. He was laughing "gleefully" and trying to get away from me. I loaded him and the duck and took him home, so relieved that he was safe. I decided that this would be a lesson to Adrian. I did not fuss at him as I could tell he was very distressed about what he had done, and he told me how sorry he was.

We had a next-door neighbor, named Sara who had retired with her husband and moved here from Mississippi. She had a great southern drawl which we all loved to hear. She had a wonderful personality and was always dressed fashionably. When she walked around the block with her husband, she was dressed in high heels with a church dress and a scarf. All her makeup had been applied, and her hair had every curl in place. The very first week she moved in, I took my children over to take a cake and introduce my family. We walked around her yard and looked at her beautiful flowers and her small vegetable garden. This was where I saw the first cherry tomatoes I had ever seen. They were still green and growing on the vine. We all admired them and she said she could hardly wait for her first crop, so she might pick them to show to her friends. As we were leaving, I told her I thought they were darling and would be anxious to see how they turned out.

A few days later, I was hanging clothes on our clothesline, and the boys were playing in the yard. We had just bought a sandbox with pails and shovels for them to play with. I looked up to see the two of them walking toward me with their pails. They were both excited, and Seth said, "Mom, we've brought you a surprise." The pails were full of the red cherry tomatoes from

Sara's garden. I said, "Boys, thank you, but these were not ours to pick." Seth said, "Mom, she doesn't like this kind. Remember she showed her green ones that she liked. We left all the green ones." I explained about what ripe meant and we knocked on her door to apologize. If she was upset, she did not show it. We became friends with her and her sweet husband for life.

Sara's yard looked so nice that I decided to start work on ours. Since I was no longer working outside the home, I decided to plant flowers around our home whenever I could. It was a beautiful day, and I had bought some bulbs to plant on the end of the house. As I walked out the door, I could hear the Great Dane across the street start to bark. He was fenced in beside his house which looked directly at the side of our house. This dog became very upset when he would see people out in their yards. We had just bought a cocker spaniel puppy and named it Dandy. I had it on a short leash and hooked it to the baby stroller where Caleb was napping. I pushed the stroller to the end of the house, carrying my bulbs and a shovel to dig up the grass where I wanted to plant them.

The Great Dane started his barking and the puppy laid down under Caleb's stroller and went to sleep. The grass I was digging was very difficult to release from the soil, so I set the shovel down and was on my knees attempting to pull it up by hand. All at once, I heard the Great Dane let out a yelp and looked up to see he had climbed the fence and was running full speed toward me and the stroller. There was no time to flee! I got to my feet just as he entered our yard. I thought he was going to attack Caleb or possibly the puppy, so I grabbed the shovel. He was lunging toward me, and the fear I was feeling did not have time to manifest itself in my body. I stepped in between the dog and stroller, just as the puppy whimpered in fear. My small son snoozed away, completely oblivious to the danger that was approaching. I pulled back the shovel, then swung it as hard as I could. I hit the dog full in the face and bloodied his nose! He was yelping as he fell to his knees and rolled over. I lost my balance and fell into the brick wall!

Both the dog and I were struggling to get up when I heard his owner coming. He was yelling at the dog and carrying a leash. I was preparing to hit the dog again, but when his owner appeared he seemed to calm down. He apologized and hooked the dog up to the leash and turned around to take him home. He did not say a word about me hitting the dog, even though the blood was dripping off his nose. I know he saw it all, as he was running toward us when I did it. I offered no apology for hitting the dog and hoped it would be fearful of me in the future. He did not ask me if I was hurt. I had skinned my bare arm and it was bleeding but I would recover. He never spoke to us again, but a few weeks later the dog was gone.

When Caleb was 4, he was playing in the yard with a neighborhood boy, James who was five. Seth was 10 and was supposed to be watching them while I took a quick bath. James' mother had just recently had her tubes tied and was resting at home while her son was supposed to be playing at our house. I had just gotten in the tub, when the bathroom door suddenly opened and there stood Caleb and James. I was trying to get covered with what bubbles there were in the tub when I said, "Boys close the door and go out to play". Caleb said, "Mom, James has something he wants to tell you. It's important." I am hiding behind my washcloth, so I said, "Okay, what is it?" James said, "My mom just got spayed." I said, "Thank you for sharing that with me. Very interesting, now go back out in the yard to play and close the bathroom door." I wondered where he gotten this description of the procedure. His dog had been spayed about a year before. Perhaps he linked the two?

Another time Seth was babysitting Caleb in the yard while I went to the neighborhood grocery. It took all of 20 minutes. When I got back home, Seth was laying on the sofa and Caleb was laughing. I asked Seth what was wrong and he said, "Look in the hall." There was a trail of vomit from the boy's bedroom window across the hall to the bathroom toilet. "What happened? Seth said, "We were playing in the yard and I felt like I needed to throw up, so I started for the back door, but Caleb got there first and locked me out. I went to our bedroom window, climbed in and threw up from the bed and across the hall to the bathroom toilet." I said, "Why didn't you throw up in the yard?" Seth said, "I thought I was supposed to throw up in the toilet." I said, "Get two buckets and two wash rags, both of you are going to clean it up". Both of them said, "Why?" I said, "Caleb is cleaning up because he locked you out of the house, which caused the mess, while Seth is cleaning up because he should have thrown up in the yard."

CHAPTER 44

ADRIAN'S FATHER'S BUSINESS

Seth was going to visit with my mother and Dad on the weekends, so everything seemed to be going in the right direction. Adrian had raised his salary some to help us adjust to my no longer having a job. He was making more money and needed to do some work on the back of his machinery business. He wanted to bring larger pieces of equipment inside so the mechanics might work on them indoors, out of the cold and heat. The roof had to be raised and the electricity had to be changed to generate enough power and light to adequately run the shop.

The business building was a large livestock barn which they were planning to use for breeding mules for World War II. It was never used due to the unexpected death of his grandfather. The barn had belonged to his mother's father and after his death, belonged to her. Adrian's father, Jan turned it into the farm equipment business. There were many barns in this town that had been converted to other businesses after the wars.

Jan had come here from Europe. He was a graduate of the Dutch Naval Academy graduating with a degree in engineering. After graduation, he served on the Holland American Lines with the rank of Second Officer. He made two trips around the world during his employment.

His parents had moved to Iowa and Michigan from Holland after World War I, because they felt it would be a safer country to live in. Soon after, Jan also moved and applied for citizenship. While reading a trade magazine, he read the need for civil engineers in the newly formed highway department, in the State of Missouri. He applied for the job and they assigned him to Southeast Missouri. While working there, he met his wife, Elizabeth at a local dance. She was a school teacher in a small town. They soon married.

During the late 1930s, Jan had the opportunity to work for an engineering company who was building the atomic plant in Paducah, Ky. This was in preparation for any coming wars, as Hitler was getting a foothold in Europe. His job ended at the end of 1941. Immediately following that, the company Jan worked for planned to send him to India to build a dam. Adrian's dad and mom had been married for 10 years and thought they were unable to have children. On December 1, 1941, after 10 years of marriage, they had twins, a girl and a boy. Jan did not want to take two infants to a country that had little health care and rejected this opportunity.

At the same time, the chance for the farm equipment business franchise happened to become available. The barn was the right size for the new business. It just needed more space and a higher ceiling for the shop. Jan never did this improvement project. Adrian thought it was time for this transition to begin.

The remodeling on the building had begun early in December, 1969, and was just a few weeks from completion. It was now January 31, 1970. There was a big snowstorm coming and extremely low temperatures were expected, so Adrian had moved the new tractors up against the building to protect them from icing and make them easier to start. One tractor that belonged to a customer had been moved inside of the shop, so that they might continue work on it the next day. The temperature was dropping dramatically, as he got into the truck to leave for home. The gray and white snow clouds were moving in. The wind was cutting right through his clothes, and the sleet and frozen snow was burning his face. He was anxious to get home for supper and a warm house.

Seth was excited about the snow and met Adrian at the door already dressed in his snow clothes. Adrian told him he was going to be awfully warm in this outfit if he kept it on overnight. He promised to get out the sled the next morning and take he and Caleb sledding, when he came home for lunch. Seth was disappointed, but after looking out the door, he decided it was too dark to go out now.

We all sat down in our small family room to watch tv. Caleb fell asleep, and we put him to bed. The three of us ate popcorn and soon, Seth was ready for bed, too. I read him his favorite book then Adrian and I said prayers with him and tucked him in. We watched the evening news and the weather report was horrible with the temperature in single digits. Following that we were in bed by 10:30 pm. We were grateful to have a warm home in this terrible weather. We both fell asleep right away.

CHAPTER 45

TRAGEDY STRIKES AGAIN

There is nothing more frightening than the phone ringing in the middle of the night. I looked at the clock and it was 1:30 am. We only had one phone, and it was in the kitchen. Adrian is a sound sleeper, so he did not hear it ring. I drug myself out of the bed and ran quickly down the hall. I was scared that this might be Adrian's mother, who was not in the best of health, or my parents! I felt drugged or as though I was in a dream. Before I could say hello, I heard a man's hurried voice say, "This is an emergency! May I speak to Adrian?" I said, "Just a moment," and ran back down the hall. I did not think to ask who he was or what he wanted. I sat down on the edge of the bed and said, "Adrian, there's an emergency and a man is on the phone for you." He sat up immediately and went to the phone. I could not hear any of the conversation, except Adrian's end of the line, but I could tell by the look on his face that it was something tragic. Adrian said, "I will be right there and hung up the phone." He turned to me and said, "Help me find my long underwear and the warmest things I have. The business is on fire and they need me to come right now!" This was so upsetting, that I had a problem finding what he needed. During the time I was searching, I heard him calling his good friend, Tim and one of his employees.

He said, "My business is on fire and I've parked all the tractors against the building. I have to get them away as soon as possible, can you come?" Both of them said, "Yes." He threw on his clothes and I said, "I'll get the boys," and he said, "No. I want you to stay here as it is too cold and too dangerous for you all." He kissed me and ran out the door. I could not go back to sleep. I could look out the window from our bedroom and see the glow of the fire in the clouds. I was worried sick and prayed for everybody to be safe and sat down to wait for the results.

Meanwhile, Adrian had pulled up to see flames shooting up the middle of the building. The firetrucks were attempting to put out the flames, but the cold weather was turning the water to ice. Fortunately, the high wind was blowing the flames away from the gas station and pumps that were on the north side of the building. Those tractors that Adrian had spent so much time parking close to the building were the main concern. We owed for all 6 of the new tractors facing the highway. The two other tractors were on the other side of the building and belonged to customers. They were in the hottest spot. One more tractor, belonging to a customer was inside the new shop and could not be saved. As soon as Adrian told the fireman his dilemma, they moved the water to the area that was the "Hot spot."

At that very moment, his friend, Tim arrived along with Adrain's employee. They rushed to the customer's tractors that were closest to the flame. Such bravery cannot be applauded enough. I don't know how they stood the temperature, as they climbed on the tractors and moved them away from the building. The next morning when we looked at these tractors, the paint was peeling off of the back, where it was so close to the intense heat. Both men seemed to be immune to the smoke and severe heat they were rushing into! Meanwhile, Adrian was trying to find some way into the office to retrieve items of his father's that would be lost forever, if he was unsuccessful. After several minutes of futile attempts, the fireman told him they had to give up trying, and Adrian rejoined his friends.

As Tim, the employee and Adrian finished the back they ran to the front. They began to try to start the new tractors to move them away from the hot wall. Adrian prayed that the motors would start, since it was so cold! Prayers were answered, as the men went back and forth, endangering their lives, to move all the tractors to a safe place. Adrian said it was unbelievable that they were able to get on the tractors, as they were so hot from the fire. The only cool spots were the fronts where the ice and snow were hitting it. The backs of the tractors were sitting against the enormous heat of the fire. There was no way to go to the back to mount the tractor, and the fronts were coated with ice from the fire hoses spray and the weather.

The wind had picked up again and the fire was becoming much larger! At this point, you could hear the groaning of the large timbers, holding the roof up, beginning to collapse! Everyone hurried to get away from the falling pieces. They just stood there and watched it as they were helpless to do anything else to save it. Two hours later, we no longer had an income. We would have to start over.

Adrian thanked Tim and the employee. They stayed a few more minutes to console him until there was nothing much left to burn. We appreciated their help so much that night and will be forever grateful. Tim has always been a good friend, and we wish there was some way we could have repaid him. We were thankful for his employee's help, who had now lost his job. Fortunately, he had no problem finding another job.

Financially speaking, we would have spent a lot of our life paying back the money for the tractors that were not covered by our insurance. What insurance we had was used to pay for the customer's tractor inside the building, the paint jobs on the other 2 that were next to the building and a few small items. The state insurance examiners were sent to do an inspection. There had recently been a lot of old barns that had been burned by an arsonist that had never been caught. Since this building had originally been a barn, it fit the same profile. Upon examination, it was found that our fire was the result of an electrical problem which originated in the area that was being renovated.

Adrian's mother was supported by this business and the building belonged to her. Any insurance money that might be left would have to go to her first. All our parts and small pieces of equipment were gone. We did not have enough insurance to rebuild nor any source of income.

I heard Adrian coming in the door and when I saw him, he was covered with soot on his face and on all his clothing. I could tell he was emotionally "wrung out" as well as physically depleted. We clung to each other, and he began to cry. He said, "Everything is gone and I feel as though I let my Father down. I told him I would take care of his business. He worked so hard for so long to get it established and now I've lost it." I said, "He would be proud of what you've done and there was no way you could have anticipated this kind of an ending. Go take a hot shower and we'll get some rest. We'll deal with this problem tomorrow." In my heart I hoped this was so, but in my mind, I had no idea where we would end up. I do believe that the Lord never closes a door without opening a window. This door had closed."

We went to bed about 5 am and had just fallen asleep. The phone rang and Adrian got up to answer it. I heard him say, "Yes sir. No sir," and then "Mr. Morris, I appreciate the offer of your business building to use but I cannot afford to rent anything right now. I have lost everything." I could not hear what Mr. Morris was saying but then I heard Adrian say, "Thank you." Then he hung up the phone. Adrian told me that Mr. Morris said, "I didn't say anything about money for the building. I am offering it to you free. He also said that he knew I would have to supply parts for the farmers equipment I had sold. They would need to have repair parts to start out the season. He could make us a loan for those parts." I told him that we had enough money in the business checking account to purchase parts, and did not want to have any further debt." I thought, "If this money goes to purchase parts, what will we have to live on? We had saved money and put in a small savings account ever since we had married. It was not sufficient to support us either." Mr. Morris was the owner of the bank that I had worked for and a very kind man.

Was the Lord opening the window? We'll have to see. That's another story.

ACKNOWLEDGMENTS

Once again, I would like to thank my eldest son and his wife for helping me to bring this book to fruition. A special thanks to my good friends, Myrna Simon from Louisiana, for coming up with the perfect title and Eky Combs of Missouri who was the ultimate Girl Scouting info provider. Much love to my husband and daughter, whose patience knows no bounds!

Two special people, Dan Petrosini, a Bestselling mystery author, has kept me informed about how to avoid online problems with people trying to "scam" you. The other is Margaret Daly, also a Bestselling author who has her own publishing and author assistant business. Margaret's vast experience and the ability to make you understand all the "ins and outs" of publishing makes her a true blessing for beginners like me.

Most of all I am grateful for all of you who have bought the book and enjoyed it. Sorry to have kept you waiting, but you will not be disappointed in the sequel. Thank you for your wonderful support!

Lydia

ABOUT THE AUTHOR

LYDIA CONSTANTINE

Lydia has always been very interested in Family History. Here, extended family have kept diaries, notebooks and merely paper accounts of the families that arrived her in the 1600's forward. These have been used for her sources until 1948 when she starts her own journey into her family story.

She is especially proud of her participation in the "Daughter's of the American Revolution." She has many patriots starting with the American Revolution followed by relative's participation in every war that has been fought through the Viet Nam War. She also has a relative that died at the Alamo.

She has a background in banking and served 23 years as the only woman on a Bank Board in her hometown. She also served as an Advisory Board Member for a National Diet Company plus owning 11 Diet Franchises throughout the Midwest and 2 Travel Agencies. Upon retiring, she accepted a job as Salesman for a new restaurant franchise which culminated in her acquiring the position of Administrative Director of the franchise. After retiring from that she spent every Tuesday with her grandchildren.

Always interested in community, as a young woman she was president of a women's Club receiving "Girl of the Year", Red Cross Chairman, winning the Southwestern Bell Award, Depot Museum President and Board Member introducing a new money raising campaign during her tenure.

She has 3 children, 5 grandchildren and 4 great grandchildren. She still plays Bridge, Golf, travels and gardens. This is the first book ever written and is a memoir under a Pen Name. The book was written for her family but she was encouraged to open it up to the public. She's not famous, but she has quite a story to tell. Tearful and funny moments. Her friends say:

"If something is going to happen, it will happen to her."

www.ingramcontent.com/pod-product-compliance
Lightning Source LLC
Chambersburg PA
CBHW070550130626
46556CB00001B/100